How to Age in Place

How to Age in Place

Planning for a Happy, Independent, and Financially Secure Retirement

Mary A. Languirand, PhD, and Robert F. Bornstein, PhD

TEN SPEED PRESS
Berkeley

In memory of Sam and Maggie Mudd,
for making it look easy

Copyright © 2013 by Robert F. Bornstein and Mary A. Languirand

All rights reserved.
Published in the United States by Ten Speed Press, an imprint of the
Crown Publishing Group, a division of Random House, Inc., New York.
www.crownpublishing.com
www.tenspeed.com

Ten Speed Press and the Ten Speed Press colophon are registered trademarks
of Random House, Inc.

Library of Congress Cataloging-in-Publication Data
Languirand, Mary A.
  How to age in place : planning for a happy, independent, and financially secure retirement /
Mary A. Languirand, PhD and Robert F. Bornstein, PhD. — First Edition.
    pages cm
  Includes index.
  1. Retirement—Planning. I. Bornstein, Robert F. II. Title.
HQ1062.L36 2013
306.3'8—dc23

                          2013005502

Trade Paperback ISBN: 978-1-60774-416-0
eBook ISBN: 978-1-60774-417-7

Printed in the United States of America

Design by Colleen Cain

10 9 8 7 6 5 4 3 2 1

First Edition

Contents

Acknowledgments

We'd like to thank a number of people who contributed greatly to this project. First and foremost, we are grateful to our agent, Joelle Delbourgo, whose support and enthusiasm over these past twelve years has been unwavering, and who helped us transform our ideas into something tangible—the book you're now holding in your hands. We'd also like to thank Julie Bennett, who had faith in our vision and signed the project, supporting us all the way. And special thanks to Emily Timberlake, whose insightful comments, questions, and suggestions helped turn *How to Age in Place* into a compelling, engaging text.

Several other members of the Ten Speed Press team made key contributions to this effort and taught us a great deal along the way. We'd like to thank Colleen Cain for her inspirational design, which complements and supports the theme of our book, and Kara Van de Water, Michele Crim, and Patricia Kelly for their invaluable contributions to publicity and marketing, helping us reach a broad and diverse readership. We are grateful to Jean Blomquist and Molly Woodward for copyediting and proofreading our sometimes challenging text, and to Ken Della Penta for providing an index that we know will serve our readers well.

Introduction
HOW WILL YOU SPEND YOUR RETIREMENT YEARS?

Kate and Tom prided themselves on being careful planners, especially when it came to something as important as retirement. They decided to retire early—Tom from his job as a professor, Kate from hers as a social worker—and since both were Civil War buffs, they bought a home in Gettysburg, Pennsylvania, near the battlefield. They decided to purchase an older house—a fixer-upper—but it was worth it because they loved the old-fashioned fireplaces, rough-hewn wood floors, antique leaded glass, and beautiful carved banisters.

Kate and Tom saved diligently for retirement and had accumulated a sizable nest egg. Now that they were living off savings rather than income, they decided to invest their funds conservatively, so they put most of their assets into a variable annuity. All went well for the first couple of years, and between trips to antique fairs and visits from their grandchildren, Kate and Tom were having the time of their lives. They went a little overboard here and there upgrading the house and property, but this was the place the kids would have forever, so it seemed money well spent.

Then the unexpected happened: Kate had a stroke. She was paralyzed on the left side. With hard work in rehab Kate recovered much of her function, but she remained wheelchair-bound and required the assistance of home health aides 24/7. A good long-term care insurance policy helped cover the costs, which was a blessing (not all long-term care policies actually cover in-home care).

As Kate worked toward recovery, problems began to emerge. Because it was an older house, there was no bath or shower on the ground floor. The doorways were too narrow to accommodate a wheelchair, and the kitchen was so small that Kate couldn't enter it at all. She was essentially a prisoner of the living room—not a good situation for someone with her busy, active personality. They explored the possibility of installing a ramp for Kate to enter and leave the house, and a lift to get her up and down the stairs, but the price of retrofitting the home was substantial.

When the stock market tanked in 2008, the monthly income from their variable annuity went from $4,000 to less than $2,400. Because they were not yet fully vested in the annuity (this typically takes anywhere from six to ten years), Kate and Tom were unable to access their funds without incurring a substantial early-withdrawal penalty. At this point, they could no longer make their mortgage payments; they were forced to sell their house at a loss. Tom moved in with their daughter and her husband, and he went back to work part-time to help cover the bills. Kate entered a nursing home. The happy retirement that Kate and Tom had long envisioned was gone.

Have you ever met anyone who wanted to spend their retirement years relying on others for help and support? Of course not. Kate and Tom certainly didn't. Like Kate and Tom, most of us plan to live at home, doing what we please, free to live out those long-deferred dreams that were put off in favor of work and raising a family.

If most of us would like to spend our retirement years at home, why don't we? Sometimes the reasons are unavoidable. Poor health may require round-the-clock nursing care; cognitive decline from Alzheimer's disease or other factors may make independent living impossible. But sometimes people can't live at home not because of health problems, but because they fail to plan ahead—they don't do the things they need to do to maintain their independence and "age in place."

What Is "Aging in Place"?

Aging in Place is a national movement aimed at enabling older adults to remain in their own homes by making available the social support, health care, and home maintenance services that people need to live safe, happy, productive lives in the community. Aging in place may mean continuing to live where you have lived for many years, or moving to a new residence (or new locale) that maximizes your ability to live independently.

Aging in place involves confronting some practical issues. If left undone, these issues can interfere with independent living:

- Financial planning
- Safe housing
- Neighborhood safety and "walkability"
- Accessibility of services (a pharmacy, for example, or nearby grocery store)
- Proactive medical and mental health care
- Opportunities for community, cultural, and civic engagement
- Sustainability to ensure long-term cost effectiveness

Beyond the practical issues, aging in place represents a philosophical shift—a social movement—which includes:

- Developing a new vision of healthy aging—a new attitude regarding needs of people in their 70s, 80s, and 90s, and the myriad ways in which older adults can contribute to society
- Creating innovative, efficient models of eldercare services that make aging in place economically viable for the individual and society

As you can see, aging in place requires some planning. But arranging those services that will enable you to live independently, safely, and comfortably, and stay active and engaged throughout your retirement, will help make aging in place the "new normal."

Kate and Tom: What Went Wrong?

Kate and Tom had planned reasonably well, and they were certainly well-intentioned, but they made two critical errors that cost them dearly in the end. First, they didn't anticipate the possibility that they might someday have to modify their home to accommodate Kate's limited mobility—and they were unaware of how costly such home modifications can be. Second, they invested the majority of their funds in a variable annuity rather than diversifying their assets. (Variable annuities can be an important part of one's post-retirement nest egg, as we discuss in chapter 1, but unlike fixed annuities their monthly payments may rise and fall with the stock market. And unlike money in a mutual fund, funds invested in an annuity cannot always be withdrawn without a substantial penalty if an emergency should arise.)

Lesson learned: Being proactive about financial planning and designing a living space where you can live safely and comfortably through your 80s and beyond are two crucial elements of aging in place—we address these issues in detail in chapters 1 and 3.

Lemons to Lemonade: Ellie's Story

Ellie had experienced her share of ups and downs. Who hasn't? But she certainly hadn't expected to go through a divorce after thirty years of marriage, nor did she anticipate that, as part of the divorce settlement, she'd lose the beautiful split-level home she'd come to love. It all seemed overwhelming at first—too much to deal with all at once—but after a bit of time had passed Ellie regained her composure. She decided to turn these lemons into lemonade, and she began to develop a plan of action.

First a place to live: With her share of proceeds from the sale of the house, Ellie bought a condo in a senior community. It was an adjustment moving to a smaller space, but she soon found that freedom from maintaining a house and property actually gave her more time and energy for other things (most senior communities provide services like lawn care and snow removal). Having comfortably downsized her lifestyle, Ellie was able to retire from her federal service job, securing a pension plus the guarantee of affordable secondary health insurance and long-term care insurance as part of her retirement package.

Never one to sit quietly as life passed by, Ellie met with a Certified Financial Planner to see what sorts of options she had with respect to her retirement savings. After investing the majority of her assets in relatively secure, conservative investments (some in mutual funds, some in an annuity, and some in CDs), Ellie mulled over various possibilities regarding what to do with the savings she had remaining. In the end, she decided to invest in Bubble Buddies, a mobile dog grooming business owned by her friend Gayle. Shampooing retrievers and clipping poodles keeps Ellie busy, but still gives her the scheduling flexibility she needs to serve on the board of directors of her church and volunteer at the local library as an adult literacy teacher.

And now she's wondering why she hadn't thought about all this years ago. . .

Financial Planning: The Bedrock of Aging in Place

They say that money can't buy happiness, and we agree, but a sound financial plan is crucial for a happy, healthy retirement. You don't need to be a millionaire to age in place, but you do need a framework that helps you make good choices about where to invest your money as retirement draws near, and a plan for how you'll "spend down" your assets when you're no longer working.

What do we mean by "spend down" your assets? It's not a term familiar to everyone. *Spending down your assets* involves developing a financial plan that allows you to draw from your accumulated savings the funds you need to pay monthly expenses—and doing it in such a way that you will be very likely to have some money (but not too much) left over when you die. A sound plan for spending down your assets is also flexible: it is structured so you can increase or decrease monthly "draw downs" as circumstances change, as new needs arise, or as the income from your investments varies due to market conditions.

Money can't buy happiness, but it can buy you autonomy, flexibility, and the freedom to live the life you want to live. Make no mistake: post-retirement expenses can be substantial—higher than many people realize. The US General Accounting Office estimates that someone turning 65 today can expect to spend upward of $200,000 in future medical costs—deductibles, copays, Medigap premiums, and out-of-pocket expenses. For those of us in our 50s, the costs will be higher, because an increasing portion of late-life health care expenses are likely to be shifted to retirees over the years as federal and state budgets grow ever tighter.

The costs of a happy, healthy retirement aren't limited to medical expenses, as Kate and Tom discovered too late. *Universal home design*—reconfiguring your space to make it safer and more accessible—can be costly indeed. Widening a doorway to make it wheelchair accessible will run several hundred dollars; installing a ramp or stairway lift can cost $10,000 or more.

The bottom line: Where post-retirement living is concerned, a sound financial plan is the bedrock that will enable you to get good health care, live independently, and do the things you want to do now that you have the time to do them.

Why Aging in Place Is Not for Everyone: Activities of Daily Living

It's important to keep in mind that aging in place is only possible if you are still able to carry out everyday tasks (like cooking, shopping, and managing money) that are critical for independent living. People who can no longer carry out these tasks (sometimes called *activities of daily living*, or *ADLs*) usually need a higher level of care—most often assisted living, but sometimes skilled nursing or nursing home care.

Health care professionals divide ADLs into two categories: basic and complex. *Basic ADLs* are skills so important that without them we could never survive on our own:

- The ability to feed oneself
- The ability to use the bathroom appropriately

- The ability to maintain acceptable personal hygiene
- The ability to dress properly for current weather conditions

To live independently, a person must not only be able to carry out basic ADLs, but also the *complex ADLs* that many of us take for granted:

- Shopping
- Cooking
- Communicating effectively with others
- Following directions
- Taking medication appropriately
- Managing money

The first signs that a person needs extra help usually involve some slippage in complex ADLs. Loss of basic ADLs comes later, and indicates a greater need for care. Of course, some injuries and illnesses can impact both, either temporarily or permanently.

With sufficient resources you can afford the kinds of in-home help that allow you to stay in your home even though you may be completely dependent on others for assistance with your ADLs (Ronald Reagan and Christopher Reeve come to mind here). But that degree of financial self-sufficiency is the exception rather than the rule.

How This Book Came to Be

The idea for *How to Age in Place* came from our earlier work in this area. Having written extensively on coping with late-life health challenges and strategies for obtaining good in-home care, we realized there was a gap—a significant gap—in the resources available to people (like us) who were starting to think seriously about post-retirement life. There was no comprehensive, user-friendly book that summarized what we all need to know to plan ahead so we can live at home, safely and comfortably, manage our finances, maintain our health, and stay active and engaged through our 80s and beyond.

So we began writing. As we wrote, we learned—and not all of it was pleasant. We discovered that our own financial plan was fine as far as it went, but it was incomplete: we had a system in place for investing, but no set strategy for spending down our assets. We discovered that our home in

> Aging in place isn't about refusing to move—it's about making mindful choices about what locale and type of housing would work best for you.

Westbury, New York, was perfect for a couple in their 50s, but not for a couple in their 70s (that stairway to the second floor seems much steeper today than when we first bought the house). As we walked through the neighborhood and tried to imagine what getting around would be like twenty or thirty years from now, we realized that our neighborhood lacked "walkability"—uneven sidewalks, too few traffic lights, busy streets that would be difficult for an older person to cross.

Full disclosure: As we did our neighborhood walkability tour, one of us—we won't say who—actually took a tumble when she tripped over a loose section of sidewalk, fell down, and skinned her knee. Apparently writing retirement books is risky business.

But we pushed on. As we wrote, we learned, and as we learned, we tested. We actually put into place the ideas that you'll read about in this book—we used them ourselves. Nothing reveals the strengths and weaknesses of a plan like trying it out for real. We've done the testing so you won't have to.

Because retirement planning is an ever-changing landscape, with new information arriving nearly every day, even the most thoroughly researched book will eventually begin to fall behind. To keep you current on the latest developments, we've created a website, www.aging-wisely.com. Our website can be your comprehensive source of information on healthy aging—we'll post updated contact information, blogs addressing new ideas and findings, and links to useful websites. We invite you to visit www.aging-wisely.com frequently and read about the latest developments.

Okay. back to the topic at hand. . .

Is Aging in Place Right for Me?

People ask us this all the time: why has aging in place become so popular? More and more retirees are choosing this option, and doing what they need to make it happen. Communities of older adults—aging in place collectives—are blossoming like wildflowers around the country, and it's beginning to gain momentum as a national movement.

So, why is now a good time to consider "aging in place"? Three reasons:

- **We're living longer, healthier lives.** Improvements in medical care, nutrition, and self-care (committing to a regular exercise regimen, for example, and quitting tobacco) make aging in place a realistic option for an ever-increasing number of people.

- **It's the most efficient way to spend health care dollars.** Every day another ten thousand Americans turn 65. By 2030, 20 percent of US residents—71 million of us—will be 65 or older. Health care resources are already stretched thin, and studies show that community-based services—services that are delivered in your home rather than a hospital or other facility—cost about 80 percent less than out-of-home care.

- **It's what people want—and do.** Recent AARP surveys indicate that 89 percent of retirees want to live at home (which makes you wonder what that other 11 percent were thinking). About 80 percent of adults between 62 and 84 own their homes outright, and only 5 percent of people aged 55+ move in a given year (versus 17 percent of under-55s). Numbers like these mean that aging in place isn't just an abstract concept—for most of us it's a possibility within reach.

Keep in mind that aging in place after you retire doesn't have to mean staying where you are if your house isn't suitable, the neighborhood has declined, or all your friends have moved. Aging in place isn't about refusing to move—it's about making mindful choices about what locale and type of housing would work best for you. So aging in place can also mean finding a new place to age. Sometimes that means moving across town; sometimes it means moving across the country.

How to Age in Place: Planning for a Happy, Independent, and Financially Secure Retirement

The goal of this book is to give you the information you need to maximize your wealth, maintain your health, and make good decisions about your environment (your home and the surrounding area) so you can age in place safely and comfortably. To guide your thinking, we developed a framework that will help you make sound retirement decisions, the access-opportunities-services (AOS) model, which we describe in chapter 2. You can use the AOS model to compare various retirement options with respect to three key criteria: access (universal home design/accessibility, availability of public transportation, neighborhood walkability), opportunities (social, recreational, cultural, educational, civic, spiritual), and services (health services, social services, nutrition services, public safety).

How to Age in Place is divided into two parts: Making It Work, and Making It Count. In Making It Work we discuss practical issues: how to fund your retirement so you can make the most of it (chapter 1), and the factors you'll want to consider in deciding where to live (chapter 2). We discuss how to modify your home to make it safer and more accessible (chapter 3), and what you'll need to know to make good decisions about transportation options, both public and private, when faced with declining mobility (chapter 4). We also discuss strategies for dealing with illness and injury when they inevitably occur (chapter 5).

Part 2, Making It Count, focuses on ways that the freedom of retirement can set the stage for continued growth and fulfillment. Here we help you live the good life into your 80s and beyond, with information on maintaining good cognitive function and maximizing your memory (chapter 6), staying healthy and exercising safely (chapter 7), and discovering (or rediscovering) life's meaning and purpose (chapter 8). The last two chapters provide advice you can use to maintain longstanding relationships and cultivate new ones (chapter 9), and ways that you can pass along to others the wisdom and experience you've acquired over the years (chapter 10).

It's never too late to begin putting your plan in place, and it's never too early either. If you're in your 60s, 70s, or 80s, the time to begin making changes is now—today. If you're in your 40s or 50s, it's time to plan for the future (and you can never start too soon). Either way, this book is for you.

PART 1

Making It Work

CHAPTER 1

Money Matters

Money matters—it's the foundation of successful aging in place. Money creates opportunities (to travel, for example, or spend more time with the kids), and it helps pay for needed services as well (like housekeeping or in-home care). A decent nest egg is crucial for a secure retirement.

But how much is enough? The answer might surprise you. Psychologists find that people who have lots of money don't report higher levels of life satisfaction than those who have what they need to manage comfortably but not much more than that. Turns out that once we've saved enough to feel reasonably secure, accumulating additional funds won't make us happier or more content.

You don't need to be a millionaire to retire well—but you do need to have a realistic sense of what your retirement expenses will be, and a plan for managing your assets so you can live comfortably and do the things you want to do. In this chapter, we address money matters. We explore whether it makes sense to continue working post-retirement or to devote your time to other pursuits. We discuss the key elements of late-life financial planning and budgeting, and strategies for setting up (then periodically adjusting) post-retirement income flow.

From Asset Accumulation to Income Stream

Many of us have devoted considerable time and energy to managing our assets—to making sure we've accumulated enough money to live comfortably, retire securely, and maybe have something left over for children and grandchildren. Asset management can be daunting during one's working years, but it's even more complicated post-retirement. Now instead of focusing only on accumulating income and maximizing investment growth, you must also consider how best to spend down your nest egg. This involves determining how much money you'll need to cover your monthly expenses, then rearranging your assets to create an income stream that allows you to meet your needs while preserving adequate rainy-day funds to deal with unanticipated events (like health crises). We actually found the "income stream" aspects of retirement financial planning more daunting than the "asset accumulation" part (creating a savings plan seemed relatively straightforward; anticipating future needs involved more guesswork).

Complicating matters—and maybe this is what threw us—you need to adjust your post-retirement spending so you don't outlive your assets, but estimating one's life expectancy is, to say the least, a bit tricky. Here you'll want to err on the conservative side: it's better to die with money in the bank than fret over expenses during your final years. More on that in a bit.

To Work, or Not to Work?

There was a time not long ago when retirement meant retirement: you stopped working altogether and took it easy. Now retirement means different things to different people, and many choose to continue working part-time, sometimes in the same field they've always worked, sometimes in a new one. There are a number of benefits, both material and psychological, to continuing to work in some capacity post-retirement. These include the additional income, social interaction, and day-to-day structure that work provides. There are some negatives too, of course, which include less flexibility in your schedule, less time for other interests (like hobbies and charitable work), and—most important of all—potential social security implications. Once your income reaches a certain level, the portion of your Social Security payments that are taxed increases, and as a result your benefits shrink. Given the tradeoff, you may find yourself working many extra hours for minimal extra income. Be sure to check the Social Security website for the most up-to-date regulations in this area (www.ssa.gov, or call 1-800-772-1213).

Whether or not to work post-retirement is an individual decision, but three guidelines can help. Bottom line—it probably makes sense to go back to work when one or all of these occur:

- **Economic conditions change or your investments go south.** If your savings (or the income they generate) have decreased to the point that you can't cover your essential expenses, you have little choice but to reenter the workforce (assuming you can find a job, which is not so easy these days).

- **You (or those close to you) have a change in circumstances.** If your financial needs change, or those of a family member increase, you might want to return to work for the extra income. If your son or daughter will have to take a second job to afford child-care costs, or your parent will need to go to assisted living without some practical assistance (like in-home health care), your retirement plans may change.

- **You discover that not working doesn't work for you (or your partner).** Japanese psychiatrists recently identified a new disorder—retired husband syndrome—that occurs when one member of a couple suddenly spends a great deal of time at home after years of long days away at the office. One intruded-upon wife in Japan actually beaned her newly retired husband with a frying pan after two weeks cooped up together (no kidding); another tried to run her husband over with the car (she missed). Many longstanding relationships need some "apart time" to thrive—too much togetherness can trigger conflict.

Once your income reaches a certain level, the portion of your Social Security payments that are taxed increases, and as a result your benefits shrink. Given the tradeoff, you may find yourself working many extra hours for minimal extra income.

>> CERTIFIED FINANCIAL PLANNERS

To use the title Certified Financial Planner, the person must have under-gone appropriate professional training and attend periodic continuing education seminars to stay up-to-date with changes in tax laws and other relevant matters. You can find Certified Financial Planners online, and in the Yellow Pages of your phone book (look under "Financial Plan-ning Consultants"). In general it's better to work with Certified Finan-cial Planners who charge an hourly fee rather than those who receive a commission for products sold, because commission-based planners may not always be objective regarding the merits (and risks) of different financial products. Two national associations can also help steer you toward reputable professionals and provide information regarding the financial planning process:

Financial Planning Association
Offices in Denver and Washington, DC
800-322-4237
www.fpanet.org

Society of Financial Service Professionals
19 Campus Boulevard
Suite 100
Newtown Square, PA 19073
610-526-2500
info@financialpro.org
www.financialpro.org

Financial Planning for the Long Term: Covering Your Ass(ets)

It's important to manage your finances carefully if you intend to age in place, but unless you have training and expertise in this area you'll eventually find yourself in uncharted territory, dealing with financial matters (like annui-ties, taxes, and trusts) that can be quite complicated. It's unwise to teach yourself the principles of asset management by experimenting with your life savings, so our most important piece of advice in this chapter is this: consult a Certified Financial Planner early in the retirement planning process. For some people, a single meeting is enough; others do best if they consult with a financial planner periodically to review their situation. Whatever you do, don't try to manage things completely on your own.

With that in mind, there are three things you should do to get started: calculate your net worth, budget for essential and lifestyle expenses, and develop a realistic time frame. Let's take a closer look at each of these tasks.

CALCULATE YOUR NET WORTH

The first step in asset management involves calculating your *net worth*—the total value of all your assets (your accumulated wealth) minus your liabilities (what you owe to others). We've provided a worksheet on page 204, and even if you've calculated your net worth already, you should probably do it again. You can catch mistakes by doing this (and besides, things change). It's usually a good idea to calculate your net worth every year or so to see how things have changed (we do it every December as the holidays draw near).

BUDGET FOR ESSENTIAL AND LIFESTYLE EXPENSES

Financial experts distinguish "essential expenses" from "lifestyle expenses." *Essential expenses* are those necessities (like groceries and electricity) that we can't live without. *Lifestyle expenses* are things like vacations and dinners out—things you enjoy, but could forego if you had to. (And no—Bruce Springsteen concerts are not considered essential expenses.)

Even if you've never created a budget before, it's helpful if you create one now so there are no unpleasant surprises down the line. We've provided a budget worksheet on page 201, and you can use it to estimate essential and lifestyle expenses. As you do this, don't forget to account for inflation, so assume that your expenses will increase gradually over time. (It's impossible to predict future inflation, of course, but in the near term—the next several years—3 percent yearly inflation is a reasonable estimate . . . 5 percent if you want to be more conservative in your planning.)

DEVELOP A REALISTIC TIME FRAME

Some guesswork is involved here, and you can never know for sure how long you'll live, but several factors will help you make a reasonable estimate:

- **Family history.** Family history is a good starting point for estimating your longevity, though it's just that—a starting point: merely because your parents both lived into their 80s doesn't mean you will too. But genes do matter, and you can get a general sense of your potential longevity (think of it as a "ballpark estimate") based on your relatives' histories. If you had parents and grandparents who lived into their 90s, then you may well have the genes that promote a long life. If none of your relatives lived past their mid-70s, you should take this into consideration when estimating your own life span.

- **Current health status.** If your health is reasonably good (no chronic diseases), and you exercise, watch your diet, don't smoke, and don't drink to excess, you've done much of what you can to help your life span approach the "high end" of its potential. If you have one or more chronic diseases (diabetes, hypertension), or unhealthy habits (eating too much, exercising too little), then your life span might be closer to the low end of the range.

- **Ask your physician.** Your physician can review your health history, and that of your family, and offer an opinion here, too. Your doctor will not only have additional perspective on your health and potential longevity, but may be able to suggest things you could do to increase the likelihood that you'll live a long and healthy life.

- **Longevity websites.** There are many longevity websites. Some are bad, but some are based on sound scientific principles and provide reasonably accurate estimates. One particularly good longevity website is www.livingto100.com.

Making It Last: Asset Management and Income Flow

According to 2010 data compiled by the US Census Bureau and Bureau of Labor Statistics, the average American age 65+ derives about 40 percent of their income from Social Security; most of the remaining income comes from post-retirement income (25 percent), pensions and annuities such as 401(k)s and 403(b)s (20 percent), and savings and assets such as bank accounts, money market accounts, and mutual funds (13 percent).

Not everyone deals with late-life finances in the same way, however. There are six potential sources available to create a post-retirement income stream: investment income, post-retirement work income, annuities, pensions and 401(k)s, individual retirement accounts (IRAs), and social security. You'll likely settle on a combination of these that suits you and your situation. Let's take a closer look at these six potential income sources.

INVESTMENT INCOME

If you've invested money in stocks, bonds, mutual funds, money market accounts, certificates of deposit (CDs), or elsewhere, you may be able to use investment income to help create your post-retirement income stream.

Some investments produce a predictable amount of income each month (CDs and savings bonds fall into this category); other investments produce income that is less predictable and more variable (mutual funds fall into this category). Many people keep a relatively high percentage of their savings in more volatile (and potentially more profitable) investments during their working years, then gradually move funds to more conservative, predictable investments as they age. You'll want to develop a strategy for shifting your investments based on the amount of money you've accumulated, the amount you'll need to pay for essential and lifestyle expenses, and other factors (like your personal investment style, tolerance for risk, and willingness to commit time and attention to your investment portfolio).

>> THE NATIONAL ACADEMY OF ELDER LAW ATTORNEYS

Elder law is the area of law focusing on the needs of older adults and their families. It includes issues such as ensuring access to appropriate medical care and social services, helping coordinate a person's resources to finance the cost of care, obtaining appropriate income assistance benefits, and dealing with matters related to taxation, estate planning, and putting in place advance directives, powers of attorney, and other legal documents.

If you can use local contacts to find a good, reputable attorney experienced in elder law, by all means do so. If you need help in locating an attorney to assist with your legal and financial preparations or simply want to obtain useful, up-to-date information on elder law, contact the National Academy of Elder Law Attorneys by mail (1604 North Country Club Road, Tucson, AZ, 85716), or via the Internet (www.naela.org).

POST-RETIREMENT WORK INCOME

As we discussed, whether you choose to work post-retirement depends upon a number of factors, including your need for structure, your desire for social contact, and—of course—the money. Post-retirement work can generate additional funds to increase your income stream or help build a rainy-day fund for unanticipated expenses.

ANNUITIES

Annuities are essentially insurance policies, though they don't seem that way when you first learn about them. You can purchase annuities through an insurance agent; be sure to work with an agent who has passed the state licensure exam, who has a current life insurance license, and who is up-to-date in his or her continuing education requirements (these vary from state to state).

When you invest in an annuity, you sign over a set amount of money (say $200,000) and receive a periodic check or direct deposit that represents earnings on your principal (say, for example, $500 per month). In most annuity agreements, you receive those periodic payments for as long as you live; if you purchase a *joint life annuity*, the payments continue as long as your partner lives as well. Some annuities are *immediate*—payments begin as soon as you invest; others are *deferred* (payments don't begin until some agreed-upon period of time has passed . . . say five or ten years). In general, deferred annuities pay a higher monthly percentage than immediate annuities because the funds have been invested longer and have had more time to accumulate. Most annuities also have a *term*—a period of time during which payments continue even if the holder of the annuity dies. Oftentimes the term is ten years, so even if you died a year after investing, your heirs would receive payments for the remaining nine years. Terms, however, vary from policy to policy, and you'll want to confirm this in writing up front.

As you can see, annuities get complicated pretty quickly. But there's more. Some annuities (called *equity indexed annuities*) are linked to the performance of a portfolio of stocks; other annuities are linked to other types of financial instruments. In a *fixed annuity*, the amount of the monthly payment is guaranteed—it's spelled out in the contract between you and the seller of the annuity. In a *variable annuity*, the payment is not guaranteed—it can increase or decrease depending upon how well the investments that comprise the annuity perform (and if things really go south the payments can shrink considerably, as Kate and Tom discovered the hard way).

>> PROS AND CONS OF ANNUITIES

Annuities have some significant advantages as a source of retirement income, and some disadvantages as well. Here are the tradeoffs:

Advantages of Annuities:

- Annuities represent a predictable source of income; most annuities have guaranteed minimum rates (often 3 or 4 percent), plus whatever additional gains your investments generate.
- Most annuities have a guaranteed payout period (called a "term"), so even if you die before the term ends, your heirs will continue to receive monthly payments.
- You can purchase a joint life annuity for additional partner protection.
- Annuities may be a good component of your overall investment package—a stabilizing influence (they're more stable than many mutual funds).

Disadvantages of Annuities:

- You can't withdraw funds from an annuity without penalty until you're fully vested (which may take six years or longer).
- Annuities often generate less income than other types of investments.
- You're dependent on the financial stability and solvency of the company (so it's better to purchase three or four smaller annuities from different companies than one large annuity from a single company).
- Sellers receive a commission—sometimes as high at 10 percent—so there's an incentive for them to "hard sell" even if an annuity might not be the best investment for you. (Keep in mind that although annuities are regulated by state insurance commissions, they're not regulated by the SEC, which reduces government oversight and your protection.)

There's no set time to purchase an annuity; most people who invest in annuities purchase them between ages 50 and 75. The younger you are when you purchase an annuity, the lower the interest rate (because you're expected to live longer). As you might expect, joint life annuities pay lower rates than single life annuities (because there's a greater chance that at least one partner will live longer); immediate annuities pay lower rates than deferred annuities (because the payments begin sooner). The best advice we can give is that you consult with a financial planner and an attorney before you purchase any sort of annuity. Annuities can be an important part of your portfolio, and your post-retirement income stream, but because they are so complicated, it's easy to misunderstand the details, and where finances are concerned, details make all the difference.

PENSIONS AND 401(K)S

Pensions are called *defined benefit plans* because—regardless of how much money you earned during your working years—your monthly pension benefit is defined (that is, specified) in your pension contract. 401(k)s (which are named after an obscure passage in the federal tax code) are called *defined contribution plans*, because you decide (within limits) how much you choose to contribute to your 401(k) during your working years. You usually get to decide how you want to invest your money as well, and you can put different percentages into different options made available to you by the manager of the 401(k) (for example, you might choose to invest 50 percent in stock funds, 30 percent in bond funds, and 20 percent in money market funds).

Unlike a defined benefit (pension) plan, the monthly payment you receive from your 401(k)—or its look-alike cousin, the 403(b)—is not guaranteed. It depends upon how you invested your contributions, and how well the various investments performed. It's important to review your 401(k) periodically and decide if you'd like to make adjustments in your portfolio, either by shifting funds around within the 401(k) (there are limits regarding how often you can do this), or by changing your future investment allocations (for example, by lowering the percentage of new deposits you invest in stocks from 50 percent to 40 percent).

One disadvantage of a 401(k) is that once invested, the money is "locked up": if you withdraw funds before age 59$^1/_2$ you face a stiff tax penalty unless the funds are used to purchase a first home, to pay medical expenses, or are withdrawn after you become disabled. Beyond this one

>> AVOIDING FINANCIAL SCAMS

Scamming retirees is big business. Sadly, but understandably, many victims are too embarrassed to admit they've been scammed, and even a successful prosecution rarely results in recovery of lost money.

Regardless of how vigilant you are, you can't protect yourself from every crook and con artist out there. But you can follow some common-sense tips that apply to *all* consumers, regardless of age:

- Get information about goods or services in writing, and review the information carefully before making a decision. Don't sign anything until you're completely satisfied.

- Be especially wary of door-to-door, telephone, or Internet salespeople. *Cold calls* (offers initiated by the seller, not the buyer) are notoriously bad risks. Do not be afraid to hang up the phone or refuse to open the door: many people have lost huge sums of money by being polite.

- Don't give out any personal information (Social Security, bank account, or credit card numbers) over the telephone or Internet unless *you* initiated the contact. Even then be careful, and make sure the recipient has a legitimate need for the information.

- Be suspicious of sweepstakes, contests, free gifts, and free vacations—anything that sounds too good to be true probably is. If a gift giver or sweepstakes representative asks for money or personal information up front (credit card numbers, Social Security numbers, and so on), it's a scam. Hang up.

- Don't assume people are who they say they are. Insist that service providers, law enforcement officials, and government representatives (like census workers or tax assessors) show proper identification *before* they enter your home. If you don't feel comfortable, don't let them in.

disadvantage, however, 401(k)s have three great advantages as a mechanism for retirement investing. First, up to a yearly limit, the money you put into your 401(k) is pretax—it actually reduces your taxable income in the year in which you invest the funds. Second, earnings accumulate tax deferred—you don't pay federal or state taxes on 401(k) earnings until you withdraw them (you must begin withdrawing your 401(k) funds at age 70^{1}/$_{2}$ or face a penalty). Third, many employers match your 401(k) contributions up to a point, contributing a percentage of your income (3 percent is fairly typical, but amounts up to 10 percent or more are not unheard of), as long as you also contribute some minimum amount. That's about as close to free money as you're ever going to get.

INDIVIDUAL RETIREMENT ACCOUNTS

Individual retirement accounts (IRAs) were introduced in the 1970s to allow workers not covered by an employer-sponsored retirement plan, such as a pension or 401(k), to make pretax retirement contributions on their own—in effect to set up their own personal retirement plan. Since they were first introduced, the guidelines have evolved considerably, and now many people are permitted to make pretax IRA contributions even if they're part of an employer-sponsored retirement plan. The tax advantages of IRA contributions phase out as income increases. (In 2012, a married couple filing jointly lost the IRA tax advantage altogether when their combined income reached $183,000). Even if your income exceeds the limit, however, you're still allowed to make IRA contributions—they're just after tax rather than pretax (so they don't lower your taxable income for the year in which you contribute).

> The tax advantages of IRA contributions phase out as income increases. Even if your income exceeds the limit, however, you're still allowed to make IRA contributions—they're just after tax rather than pretax.

Roth IRAs are quite different from traditional IRAs. Unlike the *traditional IRA* where contributions are usually made pretax and distributions are taxed when you take them, in a *Roth IRA* contributions come from your after-tax income (so there's no savings in the short term), but accumulations are not taxed when the money is withdrawn (so there's a potentially

>> TRADITIONAL IRAS VS. ROTH IRAS

Both traditional and Roth IRAs have their advantages. Each, however, has its downside as well.

Advantages of Traditional IRAs:

- Pretax contributions reduce one's adjusted gross income (AGI) in the years that contributions are made; the tax advantages are realized immediately.
- You can currently contribute up to $16,500 per year (more if you're 50+), and there are no income limits for most employer-sponsored 401(k)s and 403(b)s.
- Even if IRA laws change, you're unlikely to lose the tax advantage.

The Downside:

- Earnings and accumulations are taxed at standard income rates.
- There's a penalty if you withdraw funds before age $59^1/_2$ (except under certain limited circumstances).
- There are age-based distribution requirements—you must begin drawing funds by $70^1/_2$.

Advantages of Roth IRAs:

- Contributions come from after-tax income, but withdrawals (including accumulations) are tax free; you can currently contribute $5,000 per year ($10,000 for a couple).
- Unlike a traditional IRA, Roth IRA contributions can be withdrawn with no penalty at any time (there are limits on how soon you can begin withdrawing earnings).
- There are no age-based distribution requirements for Roth IRAs (so you can leave it all to your heirs).

The Downside:

- Contributions do not reduce one's adjusted gross income, and because tax advantages are deferred, you might not live to see them.
- Eligibility phases out at income limits (currently $105,000 if you're single; $167,000 for a couple).
- If IRA laws change, you could lose the tax advantage.

sizable accumulation you can use for your post-retirement income stream without having to pay taxes on the accumulated funds).

Like traditional IRAs, Roth IRAs phase out at certain income limits (these change year by year). You cannot withdraw funds from a Roth IRA within the first five years without incurring a substantial penalty, so don't contribute money you might need for essential expenses or emergencies. Recent changes in federal tax laws allow for some conversion of traditional IRAs to Roth IRAs, which requires that you pay taxes up front on any money you convert (these "conversion taxes" can be spread over two years), but you benefit from the tax-free accumulations and withdrawals later on. Up-to-date information about various IRA options is available through the IRS website (www.irs.gov; click on the "Individuals/Participants" link under the "Retirement Plans" tab).

> You cannot withdraw funds from a Roth IRA within the first five years without incurring a substantial penalty, so don't contribute money you might need for essential expenses or emergencies.

SOCIAL SECURITY

During your working years, it's likely that you (and your employer on your behalf) contributed to Social Security. Now that benefits are due, the monthly payment you receive is determined by two things: the amount you and your employer contributed (which earned you a specific number of Social Security earned income credits), and the age at which you begin receiving benefits. Social Security benefits are determined by legally mandated formulas and adjusted periodically for inflation and other factors. The Social Security Administration provides detailed information regarding benefit rules and regulations; you can contact them by phone at 800-772-1213 or online at www.ssa.gov.

The decision regarding when to begin receiving Social Security benefits is an important one. You can start receiving benefits when you turn 62, though if you do, the amount you receive each month will be reduced substantially—by 25 percent or more—for as long as you live. The only way to reverse this decision if you change your mind later is to pay back the amount you received prior to reaching your full benefits age. If you do this,

>> MAKING MONEY IN A DOWN MARKET

The 2008 stock market collapse was a wake-up call to many of us: it was startling to see how quickly (and how steeply) the value of our investments could decline. Money comes easy when stocks go up, but opportunities exist even in the worst of markets. If you transfer assets during a down market, you can sometimes reduce taxes in the short or long term, and by doing so you can make money (or at any rate cut your losses). Here are two strategies to be aware of:

- **Selling stocks at a loss.** If you own stock that is worth less than you paid for it, you may be able to sell it at a loss, take the deduction on your tax return, then repurchase the shares after thirty-one days have passed (if you repurchase them sooner than thirty-one days the IRS will disallow the deduction).

- **Converting to a Roth IRA.** When you convert a traditional IRA to a Roth IRA, you must pay the accumulated tax on your earnings when you make the switch. But if the value of the IRA is equal to or less than what you paid for it, there's no increase—no conversion tax.

the monthly amount will increase to your "normal" benefit based on contributions you and your employer made during your working years. (Keep in mind, however, that the amount you must repay can be prohibitive if you've received payments for several years before you change your mind.)

The "normal" age at which you can start receiving full benefits is determined by the year in which you were born; there's a table on the Social Security website listing years of birth and benefit start dates. If you were born in 1937 or earlier, the age is 65. If you were born between 1943 and 1955, it's 66. And it goes up from there (the age for people born in 1959 is 66 years and 10 months). Keep in mind that you don't have to begin receiving benefits on the start date listed in the table.

> You can start receiving Social Security benefits when you turn 62, though if you do, the amount you receive each month will be reduced substantially—by 25 percent or more—for as long as you live.

If you delay receiving benefits, you receive delayed retirement credits, and once you do decide to start receiving Social Security payments, your monthly amount will be higher, for as long as you live.

>> SOCIAL SECURITY DISABILITY

If you have a serious medical condition that is expected to last for at least one year, or a medical condition deemed to be terminal, you may be eligible for Social Security disability (SSD) benefits. To qualify, you must have worked and contributed to the Social Security system for some minimum period of time (usually around three years). You can check with Social Security to see if your work history qualifies, online at www.ssa.gov or by telephone at 800-772-1213.

As you might expect, the application process is complex, and it requires you to provide a great deal of information about your condition. The information is analyzed by your state's Disability Determination Service, which will try to judge the permanence of your illness, whether you are able to work in any capacity, and whether you can do the type of work you did prior to becoming ill. The standards are strict, and the determination process can be lengthy.

If you are found to be disabled, you will receive benefits beginning six months after your disability onset (payments will be made retroactively if that six-month date has already passed). The amount you receive is determined by your average lifetime earnings, and may be adjusted if you receive disability income from other sources (for example, workers' compensation payments). You automatically become eligible for Medicare benefits after you have received disability benefits for two years.

Keep in mind that although you continue to receive SSD benefits as long as you are disabled, these benefits do not automatically continue indefinitely—if your condition improves and you are deemed able to return to work, your benefits will end. You must undergo periodic reassessment by the Disability Determination Service to determine whether you continue to meet disability criteria.

Protect Yourself: Put It in Writing

It's not something any of us like to think about, but the costs of treating a serious illness can quickly devour a lifetime's worth of earnings. If your money is spent on health care (or on long-term care at home or in a skilled nursing facility), you might have little left for your family, and little left to support those causes closest to your heart.

Accidents and health problems strike without warning, so you should have several documents in place to protect your assets—and your loved ones—in case the unthinkable happens. Even if you're in ideal health, don't put it off. We put these in place for ourselves a number of years ago, and then updated them when we moved from Pennsylvania to New York in 2006. As you'll see, these documents enable you to make choices regarding key health care decisions now so your wishes are clear if your health declines or your ability to make informed decisions is ever called into question. A bit of planning can save endless problems later on.

ADVANCE DIRECTIVES

Advance directives are documents that formalize a person's wishes regarding future medical care and name an individual (or individuals) to make treatment decisions on his or her behalf. Most advance directives take one of two forms: the *health care proxy* or the *living will*.

- A *health care proxy* (also called a *durable power of attorney for health care*) delegates decision-making ability about medical matters to another individual, called a *proxy* The language used in a health care proxy should be as specific as possible—some states have disallowed health care proxies that were overly vague or ambiguous. In addition, the document should be in place before you undergo any significant medical procedure. People often emerge from surgery in a state of *delirium* (chemically induced confusion and agitation), and they need someone to make health care decisions for them until they regain their bearings. The health care proxy should be on file in the office of your primary physician, and in any facility where you are undergoing a medical procedure. It's also wise to keep a copy at home.

- A *living will* (also called a *directive to physicians*) outlines your choices regarding extraordinary measures taken to prolong life when death is imminent: you may choose which procedures you will and will not accept. Although you cannot ask that active measures be taken to end your life, you may decide whether you want to be on life support equipment such as ventilators or feeding tubes. The "imminence" of death is crucial here—the living will goes into effect only when physicians determine that the person is likely to die in the very near future. For a living will to be effective, it must be written in very specific language; vague or ambiguous wording can raise so many questions that the document becomes invalid. Your primary physician and health care proxy should both have copies. And remember: laws surrounding living wills vary from state to state, so check with your attorney early in the process.

POWER OF ATTORNEY

This is a legal document through which you (the *principal*) authorize another person (the *agent* or *attorney-in-fact*) to act on your behalf. To stay in effect when you, the principal, become unable to manage your own affairs, the document must be a *durable power of attorney* (a regular power of attorney is automatically invalidated when the principal becomes incapacitated).

A durable power of attorney can be as broad or narrow as you choose. It can allow the agent to perform all financial tasks, or simply enable the agent to pay bills, sign checks, or carry out other specific tasks named in the document. You must decide ahead of time how broad or narrow you want your durable power of attorney to be: once the principal becomes incapacitated, a durable power of attorney is exceedingly difficult to change, except through a lengthy and expensive court proceeding.

Keep in mind that a durable power of attorney does not forbid the principal from performing the tasks named in the document—it simply identifies another person who may *also* perform them. A durable power of attorney should be executed as soon as possible, because if you become incapacitated without this document in place, a rather complex court procedure will be needed to accomplish the same thing. (One important caveat: If you have assets in two or more states, you'll need a separate power of attorney for each state.)

Closing Thoughts: The Three Sacred Principles of Post-Retirement Asset Management

Now you know the basics, and—more important—hopefully you're aware of how much you don't know about the details of post-retirement asset management. To apply this knowledge effectively, use three principles:

- **Stay informed.** Not everyone can be a financial wizard, but you should understand the basics of the investments you own. And if you don't understand something, take the time to learn—read the fine print.

- **Get help.** Even the most well-informed investor cannot stay up-to-date on every new investment option and every change in tax law, so work with those who do. (Many highly educated people, left to their own devices, make horrible investment decisions.)

- **Don't be a schmuck.** Your financial adviser is not your friend—this person is working with you because that's how they earn their money. Trust your adviser but don't be naïve; merely because a person is nice to you doesn't mean they have your best interests at heart. If something doesn't feel right, or your adviser starts acting squirrely, take charge—talk to them about your concerns, and move your assets to a new adviser if necessary. (And take note: If the main reason you're not breaking ties with your current financial adviser is so you "don't hurt their feelings," that's a big red flag. You're just making excuses to avoid dealing with an awkward situation, but you must deal with it to protect yourself and your family.)

CHAPTER 2

Access, Opportunities, and Services

In this chapter, we discuss one of the most important aspects of aging in place: where to do it. We examine the range of living options, and the advantages and disadvantages of each. We also discuss opportunities for obtaining extra help and care that makes aging in place possible even when mobility limitations or other challenges make getting around difficult.

Many people think that aging in place means staying right where you are, but (to borrow a phrase from *Porgy and Bess*), it ain't necessarily so. Aging in place can also mean choosing a new setting—one that will allow you to maximize your independence and live the life you want to live for as long as possible. Sometimes this does indeed mean remaining in your current living space; sometimes it means moving once or twice as circumstances change, perhaps downsizing (for example, from a house to an apartment), and maybe relocating as well (for example, to a locale with better weather).

The Access-Opportunities-Services Model

To help you make that all-important decision about location—where to spend your retirement years—we've developed a three-step framework: the access-opportunities-services (AOS) model. The AOS model addresses three key factors that are crucial in creating a satisfying living situation. Preferences may vary from one person to another, but we all need *access* to things that enable us to live comfortably, *opportunities* to take part in interesting, fulfilling activities, and *services* that help keep us healthy and safe.

> Many people think that aging in place means staying right where you are, but aging in place can also mean choosing a new setting—one that will allow you to maximize your independence and live the life you want to live for as long as possible.

ACCESS: GETTING AROUND

Access involves being able to move around safely, within and outside your home, and being able to get the things you need to live (like groceries). As we age, access tends to become more challenging, and a house with steep stairways will be less than ideal if you're injured or ill. On the other hand, a fully accessible state-of-the-art apartment won't do you much good if the nearest grocery store can only be reached by car and you don't drive. Here are some key access issues to consider:

- **Housing.** Could you navigate your home with a walker or wheelchair? If not, what changes would be required to make this possible—a few minor modifications or complete remodeling? Can you see yourself living in your current neighborhood as an 80- or 90-year-old? If not, you might want to relocate sooner rather than later.

- **Transportation.** Is living in your current home only feasible as long as you can drive? Is there safe and convenient public transportation nearby? If travel is part of your long-term plans, think about whether you can get to the airport or train station easily, or whether you'd need to take a taxi, two trains, and a shuttle every time you want to get on a plane.

- **Shopping.** Are the stores you need for everyday living close by? A quaint historic town might seem like a great spot to retire, but if there's only one grocery store, you may find yourself without easy access to your favorite brands (no Dingle Dogs!). A big city setting brings a different dilemma: a wide range of choices, but if your budget is tight, all those choices are just a frustrating tease.

>> AGENCIES ON AGING

Most counties in America have a local Agency on Aging (AOA), staffed with people who serve the needs of community members age sixty and over. Their mission is simple: to allow older adults and people with disabilities to "live with dignity and choice in their homes and communities for as long as possible."

Initially created in 1973 following passage of the Older Americans Act, your local AOA can be a tremendous resource, advocating for retiree-friendly programs at the local, state, and national levels, and coordinating social services within the community (everything from Meals on Wheels to elder abuse prevention). AOA staff are available to answer questions and address problems (within reason), and you should feel free to use their services—it's your right. You may also want to consider getting involved in your local AOA as a staffer or volunteer; agencies encourage those who receive their services to take part in the action.

AOA staff members are often extremely devoted to their clientele: when we sat on the Citizen's Advisory Council of the Adams County (Pennsylvania) AOA back in the 1990s, the director took a personal interest in every individual who sought services—so much so that he would often make after-hours home visits to people living alone if they hadn't checked in with the agency in a while.

You can contact your local AOA by phone (they should be listed in the Human Services section of the phone book), or call the National Association of Area Agencies on Aging at 202-872-0888. You can also reach them online at www.n4a.org, or by mail at 1730 Rhode Island Avenue NW, Suite 1200, Washington, DC, 20036.

OPPORTUNITIES: OUT AND ABOUT

Being able to do the things you want is the whole point of aging in place. For some people, proximity to a bike path or park is crucial; for others, it's theaters and concert halls. Many people know exactly what activities they like, but for some of us (especially those who spent decades focusing on work and little else), knowing how we want to spend our leisure time can be surprisingly challenging. Here are some questions to ask yourself:

- **Social and recreational.** Do your plans include spending time with old friends? Making new ones? *Cohort living* (living among people one's own age) makes socializing easier, and ups the odds that appropriate recreational venues will be nearby.

- **Cultural.** Does your planned setting have venues for movies and plays? Is there easy access to libraries and bookstores? Making sure there's a good fit between what you want and what's offered matters, too. A classic rock aficionado may not be thrilled by the Grand Ole Opry, nor will the fan of cutting-edge indie films be excited by the offerings at the average suburban multiplex. Larger questions of culture enter in here as well: do you want to live among people from diverse religious and ethnic backgrounds, or are you more comfortable surrounded by peers whose upbringings are similar to your own?

- **Educational.** For many people, learning is a lifelong pursuit. Is there a college or university with adult education programs nearby? Does the local library offer classes of interest to you? If your plans involve honing your cooking skills or learning to speak Mandarin Chinese, consider whether your setting will give you access to people with expertise in these areas.

- **Engagement.** Many people see their retirement years as the chance to mentor others, become politically or socially active, or get involved in local government (more on that in chapter 10). Will your retirement setting offer the chance to remain engaged in these ways? If you're happy being a reader at the local library's weekly story hour, a small town may offer all the engagement opportunities you need. If your plans are on a grander scale, a different setting is required.

- **Religious/spiritual.** Some people can worship anywhere and any-time, while others prefer more structured, formal services with like-minded congregants. If you are in the latter group, you might be uncomfortable in a retirement community associated with a faith dif-ferent from your own, or in a small town where there are no houses of worship affiliated with your religion.

SERVICES: GETTING WHAT YOU NEED

Making sure you can get the services you need is one of the most significant challenges of aging in place. Sometimes needed services are there, but they're physically inaccessible or financially out of reach. Sometimes the service infrastructure in a particular area is inadequate—the services sim-ply don't exist. Here's what you should consider:

- **Health.** It's no secret that medical problems tend to increase with age, and they tend to become more complicated as well. The general practi-tioner who once served all your health needs may now be joined by the cardiologist, the endocrinologist, the podiatrist, the oncologist, and the urologist. Even if you have easy access to a physician you know and love, if your preferred provider opts out of your insurance plan's panel, you could find yourself living next door to services you cannot afford to use.

- **Social services.** Most communities have a Social Security branch office, senior center, Meals on Wheels, and other social service providers within reasonable reach. However, if your circumstance requires more help than is available in the area, you may have difficulty obtaining the services you really need. (Even if your community offers Meals on Wheels, they might not be equipped to accommodate a specialized renal diet.)

- **Safety issues.** Many communities offer medical alert systems, which allow you to summon help if you're in distress with the push of a but-ton, and almost all communities have 911 services, but don't forget the subtle safety issues that can easily go unnoticed. A mountainside home may be tricky in winter if vehicles (including ambulances) can't make it up the snow-covered road. It's one thing to haul your trash to the end of a long driveway when you're 40 but not so easy when you're 70.

- **Legal/financial.** Many communities offer a variety of assistance pro-grams for older adults (tax relief, for example, and help with heat and electricity costs), but here the devil is in the details. Your area may advertise attractive tax breaks for retirees while neglecting to men-tion the stringent eligibility criteria. Or there may be a waiting list for certain programs.

- **Personal.** If you're considering relocating, it's wise to think about how you'll replace some of the essential service providers in your life—the dentist you've come to trust, for example, or the hairdresser you've known for the past twenty years. If you're a creature of habit, these "minor" changes can have a major impact on your quality of life.

Housing Options

For a brave few, retirement is an opportunity to hit the road, crisscrossing the country in an RV, or (for the truly fearless) on a motorbike. For most of us, however, the locations where we choose to age in place are more traditional: the private home, condo or co-op, or other fixed residence. In the sections below, we discuss the array of housing options available to age in place. Each option has its own distinct advantages, so you'll want to choose the one that best suits your needs.

PRIVATE HOME

Most people of retirement age—upward of 80 percent in most surveys—live in houses they own. Many older adults have lived in the same house for many years, often in the community where they grew up. While these trends may be shifting somewhat in response to various social and eco-nomic factors, they remain true today for the majority of retirees.

Having lived in the same house for years gives you immense familiar-ity with it. This alone helps make your house a safe environment: even if memory fades a bit and eyesight begins to fail, you could probably navigate the entire place flawlessly from sheer repetition and habit. You've also had ample opportunity to position furnishings and possessions exactly as you like them. Emotional associations have layered there as well—a wall is not merely a wall, but the spot where you marked your children's heights or displayed a hard-earned diploma.

The thought of changing your comfortable nest may seem unthinkable, but a few relatively minor renovations can make a major difference in safety. Ramps can be added to make entries wheelchair accessible. Doorways can be widened, grab bars and shower seats installed to prevent bathroom slips and falls. New lighting fixtures make rooms brighter (and

>> CHOOSING YOUR RETIREMENT LOCALE

People choose retirement locales for all sorts of reasons, some personal (like proximity to family), others more general (like weather). Below we've listed some of the most common options based on the sorts of opportunities they provide. We realize this list is a bit artificial: some places don't fit neatly within any category, and some meet multiple criteria (for example, coastal Maine is scenic and also brings you proximity to activities like sailing and fishing). Cohort living (see Senior Community, page 43, and Naturally Occurring Retirement Community, page 46)—formal or informal—can take place just about anywhere. So this list below isn't meant to be exhaustive, but just to get you thinking about possibilities:

- **Urban.** Some retirees opt for urban settings—large cities (like New York) or smaller ones (like Cincinnati). Typically, an urban setting means apartment living, walkability, access to a wide variety of cultural opportunities, and (hopefully) decent public transportation.

- **Suburban.** In most suburban areas, walkability is limited—you'll have to access many goods and services by car. If you live near a commuter bus or train line, you can combine the extra space that usually comes with suburban living with access to urban cultural resources like concerts and museums.

- **Historic.** Gettysburg, Pennsylvania, has always attracted a large number of history buffs and retired military families; Sharpsburg, Maryland, would also fall into this category.

save energy in the process). Accessible appliances can be purchased, counters lowered, and flooring replaced to smooth out buckles and bumps. And all these things can be done without changing the essential character of the home you've come to love. Even better, some of these renovations may be tax deductible, or among the "excludable" assets (assets you're allowed to hang onto) during the Medicaid spend-down process. Such tax breaks and exclusions help trim costs considerably. (In chapter 3, we discuss the

- **Scenic.** Places like Sedona, Arizona, and the Napa Valley in California belong in the scenic group; we had a friend who moved to Missoula, Montana, for this reason as well. (Though after a couple of tough Montana winters, she relocated to a more temperate climate.)
- **Activity focused.** Some retirees choose settings based on the availability of a particular activity (like boating or skiing).
- **Education focused.** Increasingly, colleges and universities are offering educational programming designed specifically for retirees, and many retirement communities are building educational opportunities into their pitch.
- **Culture focused.** We have a colleague—a skilled violinist—who's retiring to Stockbridge, Massachusetts, because of the region's extensive concert schedule. Other culture-focused retirement opportunities might involve access to museums, theater, or dance.
- **Cohort living: formal.** Here we're talking about settings like senior communities and continuing care communities—places specifically designed with older adults in mind. If living among age mates is important to you, this is one way to ensure that you'll be surrounded by peers.
- **Cohort living: informal.** A naturally occurring retirement community (NORC) would fall into this category, as would a group of friends who simply choose to retire close by each other.
- **Weather based.** That's why Florida has long been popular—and increasingly retirees are looking westward as well, to Arizona and New Mexico.

various structural and surface modifications you should consider to make your home as safe and comfortable as possible.)

APARTMENT, CONDO, AND CO-OP

Owning a condo or co-op is much like owning a house: if you've lived there for a while, you gain all the benefits of familiarity. And like a private home, you can modify a condo or co-op to suit your changing needs. Even if you rent rather than own, you can render your living space safer with grab bars, railings, and other accommodations. In some cases, landlords who receive federal or state funding are legally required to help pay for these alterations (they might not be keen on telling you this, though, so ask).

In at least two respects, apartments are even better than houses for aging in place. For one thing, there's no grass to mow or snow to clear. Apartments also have the advantage of neighbors close at hand, and if your building happens to have doormen or maintenance staff on site, these are additional eyes, ears, and helping hands. (Keep in mind that building staff aren't trained or paid to be caregivers, and—quite understandably—most are not comfortable in that role.)

ELDER COTTAGE HOUSING OPPORTUNITY (ECHO)

The "mother-in-law" apartment/cottage option (in Great Britain they call them "granny flats") has become much more common in recent years, as families pool financial resources during tough economic times. Traditionally, a mother-in-law apartment is a room or rooms that are added to a family's existing home so that aging parents or in-laws can live with their younger family members. ECHO cottages—small freestanding buildings that include bedroom, bath, and kitchenette—are becoming increasingly popular, though, since many families prefer a separate cottage with increased privacy that still allows for physical closeness and quick access in case of an emergency.

ECHO cottages can be surprisingly economical as well: around $25,000 for a basic prefab 500-square-foot unit with few frills, to $100,000 or so for a high-end cottage with all the bells and whistles. A recent variation on the ECHO flat called the MEDCottage is a portable prefabricated 12 by 24-foot high-tech cabin that sells for between $65,000 and $75,000, and includes modest living quarters (similar to an ECHO cottage), along with a built-in monitoring system that transmits the occupant's vital health information to caregivers.

Because mother-in-law apartments and freestanding cottages both require construction of new living space and modification of existing property (including pouring the foundation and running plumbing and electric from house to cottage), they are subject to state and local zoning laws, which can sometimes be byzantine. Working with an attorney knowledgeable in local construction regulations is helpful here. Keep in mind that ECHO modifications, once made, can be difficult to undo, and may have significant impact on the saleability of the property. Nonetheless, for many people, the ECHO option is a perfect way to blend closeness and access with privacy and independence. And because they require outdoor space, ECHO cottages are really only suitable in suburban and rural areas.

SENIOR COMMUNITY

The typical senior community is a grouping of modern, accessible apartments, townhouses, or small private homes limited to people over 55. Although senior communities have historically been quite inflexible regarding minimum age requirements, the Great Recession of 2008 forced some communities to bend the rules temporarily, admitting younger residents to fill their available spaces. Now the rules have started to tighten again, and it won't be long before the under-55s who entered these communities reach the same age as most of their neighbors.

Senior communities exist to provide same-generation (or "cohort") living spaces for relatively healthy, independent older adults who don't want to live near children or teenagers. Traditional multigenerational families are not welcome, though as people live longer, it is not unusual for siblings, in-laws, or two generations of a family—all age 55 or older—to live in the same community.

Most senior communities have strict rules intended to maximize the safety and peace of the residents. Younger guests may visit briefly, but the duration of their stay is limited to a few days at a time—sometimes a week or two, not much more than that. Cats may be allowed; dogs might not be (and if they are, they must be kept indoors). Because of age restrictions

>> FRIENDS OR FAMILY?

Studies show that about half of older women and 20 percent of older men live alone at some point. Many people report reasonable satisfaction with solo living, but sometimes the challenges can be daunting, especially for those who are less outgoing or less comfortable tackling the unfamiliar. If you live alone or your partner predeceases you, two options still allow you to surround yourself with others.

Living with Family

Assuming your family gets along reasonably well, this option has many advantages. Old and young have the opportunity to learn from one another and reconnect. Younger family members can teach older ones new technologies and help out with household tasks. Older family members pass along wisdom, insight, and family history; they can also provide child care while younger family members are at work or at school.

There's a downside as well: longstanding relationship issues have no expiration date, and resentments and tensions tend to increase when space is shared. Adjusting to life in one's children's (or grandchildren's) home may also mean getting used to rules that seem strange or go against your values ("She's staying out past midnight? She's only 19!"). And some potential conflicts are deeper than one's values and preferences. Much as you love babies, you may not be physically ready for the sleep deprivation and illnesses that inevitably accompany them.

and admissions criteria, residences cannot be passed to relatives or friends like a typical house or condo, which limits the appeal of senior community housing for some people. While many senior communities allow residents to hire in-home care as the need arises, some require that the residents leave the community if they develop chronic health problems that would compromise safe independent living.

There are three main advantages to senior communities. The first involves services—most senior communities do lawn care, home maintenance, and snow plowing for you. Some also provide transportation to and from shopping areas and other commercial hubs. A second advantage

Living with Friends

In some cases, friends—of the same gender or otherwise—who find themselves in similar situations join forces to share costs and companionship. Some communities have developed formal "shared housing" programs that introduce people with extra living space to those in need of a place to live, to facilitate mutually beneficial matchups. (You can get great information regarding shared housing programs in your area from the National Shared Housing Resource Center, accessible on the web via nationalsharedhousing.org; they provide links to websites of seven national regional centers and one international resource center, and you can click through the Program Directory link to see a listing of shared housing programs by state.) As with all roommate situations, it's a good idea to put the key aspects of your shared-space agreement in writing so there are no unpleasant surprises regarding obligations and expectations.

Those who've tried living with friends often report that the trickiest aspects of the arrangement relate to dealing with each other's visitors, particularly when both of you want to use some scarce resource at the same time. Compromise on everyone's part is important here, and, if necessary, a schedule for shared space can be created to minimize conflicts and misunderstandings.

involves opportunities (cultural and otherwise); by focusing exclusively on the 50+ crowd, senior communities can tailor programs and perks to the preferences and needs of the residents (think bridge lessons or bowling leagues rather than "Mommy and Me" classes).

A third advantage of a senior community is "cohort living"—being surrounded by people your own age, with similar life experiences. Because of their strict rules and regulations regarding who may move in—or visit for more than a day or two—senior communities may be good choices for people who prefer a quiet locale to one that is more active (and potentially noisy).

NATURALLY OCCURRING RETIREMENT COMMUNITY (NORC)

Naturally occurring retirement communities (NORCs) consist of retirement-age folks who choose to live together or close by one another, and share living expenses, transportation services, housekeeping services, and sometimes caregiving services as well. Guidelines vary from state to state, but in general a NORC is a neighborhood where most residents are 55 or older (sometimes a NORC may be contained within a single apartment building, but the concept is the same). In contrast to a planned senior community, which is usually run by a corporation, NORCs evolve naturally as people who've lived in the area for years (or decades) age. Once 80 percent of the residents in a building or neighborhood reach age 55, the community automatically attains NORC status. At that point, residents can file documents that allow the community to be officially recognized as a NORC, and once those documents are in place no under-55s may move in.

NORCs have certain economic and legal advantages. Sometimes NORC members band together as a "purchasing bloc" to buy in bulk, qualify for group discounts, and negotiate reasonable rates for lawn care, snow removal, and other essentials. In some NORCs, members act as durable powers of attorney for healthcare or finance so members of the group can make unpleasant but necessary decisions (for example, decisions regarding hospice and end-of-life care) for each other as the need arises. While completely legal (assuming the proper documents have been filed), it's important to keep in mind that these power of attorney arrangements are not always respected by health care providers and other authorities, who tend to be uncomfortable dealing with nonfamily members in such situations. If you've appointed friends rather than relatives to make health care or financial decisions for you, be sure to tell your physician and attorney about your wishes while you're still well, and ask them to make a written note in your chart or file to minimize misunderstandings at critical times.

> Once 80 percent of the residents in a building or neighborhood reach age 55, the community automatically attains NORC status. At that point, residents can file documents that allow the community to be officially recognized as a NORC, and once those documents are in place no under-55s may move in.

Helping Hands

For many people hands-on help is required for successful aging in place. Sometimes all you need is someone to shovel snow or carry the groceries—task-specific and time limited. Or you might require help dressing or getting to the bathroom safely; now we're talking services that are a bit more formal.

The more complex your needs, the harder it will be to find someone close by who can meet them. Even if the people with whom you live are eager to lend a hand, they may not have the skills and training to help you effectively (or be strong enough to lift you if you fall). Bottom line: If you need help with the more basic activities of daily living (like dressing, bathing, or using the bathroom) and you don't want to leave your home, you'll need to find in-home care.

If you've appointed friends rather than relatives to make health care or financial decisions for you, be sure to tell your physician and attorney about your wishes while you're still well, and ask them to make a written note in your chart or file to minimize misunderstandings at critical times.

The good news is, in-home care is easy to find: there are many certified home health care agencies and independent providers happy to provide these services. The bad news is that this type of help is often fairly expensive, as it is not covered by Medicare or private health insurance. Home health care costs vary by region, with hourly rates in 2012 ranging from about $25 (in Arkansas, Indiana, and Kentucky), to more than $50 (in Alabama, Alaska, and Washington). The US average is about $35 per hour right now (though that figure will likely increase over time). In-home caregivers come in two varieties: the certified home health care agency and the independent provider.

THE CERTIFIED HOME HEALTH CARE AGENCY

A certified home health care agency is a corporation that employs a range of in-home health care service providers. To become certified, the agency must meet stringent federal and state standards in a variety of areas. Certified home health care agencies can be found through your physician,

>> AGING IN PLACE COLLECTIVES

It's like the 1960s all over again: a group of idealistic, civic-minded friends come together to create a community of shared values, goals, and dreams. But now the psychedelic VW bus has been replaced by a fuel-efficient midsize, the pot has given way to Geritol, and everyone is on a special diet. (Okay, we're just kidding—some of these organizations are actually pretty groovy. Check out www.intentionalagingcollective.blogspot.com; it's full of useful, inspirational tidbits.)

The basics of aging in place collectives are straightforward: they involve groups of older adults who live in close proximity; make formal, written arrangements to look out for each other; and pool their resources to increase their purchasing power and their voice in local politics and community affairs. Most aging in place collectives have yearly membership fees, which vary from community to community, but are generally in the range of $500 per year for an individual, and $750+ per year for a household. Often there are sliding scales so less well-off members pay lower fees. In return, you gain access to various amenities, which may include:

- Meal programs and nutritional counseling
- Collective neighborhood care (like shared lawn care)
- Transportation to and from appointments
- Cultural and wellness programming
- Simple home repairs (and sometimes help with computer glitches)
- "Check in" calls for members who live alone

your private health insurer, Medicare, the local chapter of the Visiting Nurses Association of America (202-384-1420 or vnaa.org), area hospitals and nursing facilities, your local Agency on Aging, and the National Association for Home Care & Hospice (202-547-7424 or www.nahc.org).

Certified home health care agencies must make their customer satisfaction data (ratings by past care recipients and their families) available to anyone who requests it, and reputable agencies are usually happy to share this information with you. In fact, if you ever encounter resistance when you request information in this area, that's a big red flag—look elsewhere.

In choosing an agency, be ready to provide detailed information about the services you seek, and ask specific questions about how well they can meet your needs. Ask how long they've been in business, and request the names of doctors and other service agencies with whom they work closely. Ask how they recruit and reward good staff, and their procedures for addressing problems or complaints. Ask whether they can guarantee full coverage for holidays and vacations. We provide a checklist on page 210 that you can use to evaluate home health care agencies on key dimensions, and compare different providers.

THE INDEPENDENT PROVIDER

Not all caregivers choose to work for agencies; some prefer to offer their services privately, deciding for whom they will work on a case-by-case basis. When dealing with an individual rather than an agency, keep in mind that you may have to do more of your own leg work to ensure coverage for those times when that person is unavailable (holidays, for example, or times when the provider has issues of her own to deal with).

Independent providers of home health care can usually be located through the same channels as certified home health care agencies. Because they are not subject to the same stringent federal and state standards as agencies, however, you'll have to rely more on your own judgment in choosing whether an independent provider is right for you. So do four things:

1. **Meet with the provider personally.** There's nothing like a face-to-face interaction to help evaluate a potential caregiver.

2. **Review their references and credentials.** Everything should be in order here—no exceptions, no excuses.

3. **Ask others about the provider's performance.** Past clients are a great source of input.

4. **Trust your instincts.** If something feels wrong, it probably is.

>> LONG-TERM CARE INSURANCE

If you can afford it, long-term care insurance is a great tool for extending the time you'll age in place, even if faced with cognitive and physical decline. Keep in mind that long-term care insurance policies vary greatly, both in what they cover and how easy it is to make changes once the policy is set up. A good long-term care policy doesn't just help pay for nursing home care; it helps pay for in-home health care and custodial assistance as well.

For most people, the optimal age to purchase long-term care insurance is in your mid-50s—close enough to retirement age that you won't end up paying premiums for longer than necessary, but still early enough that premiums are affordable (the older you are when you purchase long-term care insurance, the higher the monthly premium will be). A word of caution for those who are at risk for chronic conditions like diabetes, either because of family history or a less-than-healthy lifestyle: be sure to purchase long-term care insurance before your health begins to decline; once you've developed a serious, chronic illness like diabetes, long-term care insurance may be virtually impossible to acquire—or prohibitively expensive.

Long-term care insurance benefits are usually triggered by deterioration in ADLs (activities of daily living), as determined by one's primary physician. This can be tricky, though—some policies will only pay for services if you need help with three or more ADLs—for example, dressing, cooking, and bathing (deterioration in two areas is not enough). And some policies only pay benefits when the recipient is *physically* incapable of performing these tasks—if ADL deterioration stems from cognitive decline (like Alzheimer's disease), the insurer won't pay. If possible, look for a policy that:

- Allows the holder to receive benefits when they need help with only one or two ADLs

- Includes mental competence considerations (these policies allow coverage when the recipient cannot perform a task due to confusion or dementia)

- Offers flexibility and choice regarding where and by whom services may be provided
- Covers a broad range of services, including skilled nursing care, intermediate care, custodial care, adult day care, in-home care, and respite care
- Has few (or no) exclusions for preexisting conditions
- Does not require a hospital stay to trigger benefits
- Offers inflation protection, is guaranteed renewable, and has "step-up" and "step-down" options (these allow the holder to change coverage as his or her needs change)

As you can see, careful shopping is crucial when buying a long-term care policy. Premiums are expensive (usually $500 per month or more), and coverage stops when you can no longer pay premiums (for this reason, experts recommend that premiums not exceed 5 percent of your after-tax income). According to year 2011 industry standards, long-term care policies are best suited to those whose "nonexcludable" assets are in excess of $200,000, and whose annual income is $30,000 or more. Fortunately, the IRS does allow a certain portion of one's long-term care insurance costs to be deducted from earned income, which helps quite a bit, especially for retirees on modest or fixed incomes. Deductible limits vary by age, and are adjusted each year. In 2011, they ranged from about $1,200 for people aged 51 through 60, to $4,200 for those 70 or older.

> Unlike Medicare or private health insurance, most long-term care insurance policies cover some custodial or nonskilled services (such as light housekeeping and transportation).

Long-term care insurance is important—and complicated—so read the policy carefully before you buy, and get advice from a financial adviser who can assess your holdings and determine whether you might do better investing the money you would have spent on premiums, earmarking it for medical needs.

In addition to reviewing references that address such traits as reliability, competence, and judgment, look for a professional appearance, quiet self-confidence, good observation and communication skills, and a sense of humor—all important qualities in an independent provider.

PAYING FOR IN-HOME CARE

Not surprisingly, in-home care can be expensive: in 2011, the average cost for four-day-per-week in-home care was more than $24,000 per year. So how can you fund these services? For many people, the best option may be a long-term care insurance policy. Unlike Medicare or private health insurance, most long-term care insurance policies cover some custodial or nonskilled services (such as light housekeeping and transportation). Eligibility criteria (which often include waiting periods and dollar amount exclusions) differ from policy to policy; you should check with your insurer for details before you contract for services or file for benefits. Some states have subsidized programs that fund in-home care as a way of delaying nursing home placement (which is far more expensive); check with your local Agency on Aging to find out if your community offers this option.

Looking Ahead

We'll discuss key aspects of access, opportunities, and services in greater detail in the next several chapters. To get things started, we've provided a checklist of the major access, opportunity, and service considerations—the key questions you want to ask in each area—and you can use this checklist as you plan. We suggest you make copies of the checklist (see page 206) and bring them along with you so you can make notes as you evaluate and compare various living options.

With checklist in hand, let's begin. Chapter 3 discusses one of the most important considerations in aging in place: safe living.

>> ASSISTED LIVING

We know: it seems like the first step toward a nursing home, a slippery slope from which there's no turning back. But that's not true, and you shouldn't rule out assisted living until you're familiar with its pros and cons. Assisted living provides room, board, laundry and housekeeping services, and limited help with basic ADLs such as bathing or dressing. While some assisted living facilities have private rooms, many are semiprivate, with a shared bath. Meals are served in communal dining areas. Transportation is often available (although there may be an additional fee). Some settings offer programming and recreation; community rooms and special function rooms (such as game rooms) may also be available for resident use. Median annual costs for a one-bedroom unit in an assisted living facility tend to run about $45,000 per year, according to 2011 figures.

All assisted living facilities are staffed 24/7 by licensed health professionals (usually registered nurses or licensed professional nurses), and many offer personal medical alert systems. Depending on state rules and regulations, some may offer help with medication management and basic health monitoring (for example, blood pressure or blood glucose monitoring). Most assisted living settings cannot manage residents with complex health care needs such as incontinence or advanced dementia, and most require that the resident relocate to a higher level of care if such conditions develop. There has been increased flexibility in this area in recent years as more assisted living facilities try to accommodate people with advanced medical problems who need higher levels of care.

Like many settings, assisted living gets mixed reviews from those who've been there. While some residents liken assisted living to dorm life, many voice the same complaints heard among nursing home residents: lack of privacy, autonomy, and choice. Strict rules about food and food preparation items (such as microwaves or coffeepots) in rooms tend to be a major sticking point, while residents with higher levels of care needs sometimes complain of slow staff response times and inadequate assistance. Adaptable people sometimes adjust fairly well to assisted living, but many residents report feeling as though they are stuck in a transitional state, neither fully independent nor sufficiently cared for, and for such people the facility never quite feels like home.

CHAPTER 3

Making Your Home Safe

Kate and Tom's disastrous experience in post-retirement living stands as a cautionary tale, with an important take-home message: hope for the best, but plan for the worst. Unanticipated events can disrupt even the best-laid plans, and it need not be something as serious as a stroke. We know a couple who were visiting friends in Michigan, and one misplaced step—she thought she'd reached the bottom stair, but she hadn't—led to a trip and fall, dislocated knee, two surgical procedures, and more than eight months of rehabilitation before she was truly mobile again.

The bottom line: Safe living begins with choosing where you'll spend your retirement years, but it doesn't end there. Once you've made that decision, you should take a good hard look at your home so you can think about how you'd modify your environment to accommodate changing needs. Safe living also means planning for those aspects of your environment that cannot be altered (like weather conditions), and thinking about how you would deal with unanticipated problems (like failing memory) before they occur.

These preparations are not only critical for being safe, but for feeling safe as well. Peace of mind is priceless.

Making Space Accessible: Universal Home Design

Universal home design is the term used to describe living spaces that people with various challenges (physical, sensory, cognitive) can use on their own—living spaces that enable them to carry out ADLs (like cooking and cleaning) effectively. Access—the first component of the AOS model—is a key consideration here, and while it's easier to implement principles of universal home design when a space is first built, existing homes can often be "retrofitted" to suit.

On page 212, we've provided a checklist of common universal home design modifications you should consider. They range from changes involving the exterior of your home (like smoothing pathways for increased accessibility), to plumbing adjustments (like installation of antiscald controls), and everything in between. As you can see, the list is long. We're not suggesting that you make every one of these changes to age in place successfully, but you should be aware of all the possibilities, and weigh the costs and benefits of each.

Let's look at a few of the most important universal home design issues in more detail.

> *Universal home design* is the term used to describe living spaces that people with various challenges (physical, sensory, cognitive) can use on their own—living spaces that enable them to carry out ADLs (like cooking and cleaning) effectively.

ENTRANCES, HALLS, AND STAIRWAYS

Stairs, raised doorsills, and narrow doors and hallways render an otherwise ideal space completely off-limits to people in wheelchairs, and tricky for those who use walkers. Doorways can be widened (36 inches is the minimum width to accommodate most wheelchairs), and fitted with lever handles and easy-to-reach locks. Raised doorsills can be evened out by a universal home design specialist.

According to Home Safety Council statistics, older adults in the United States experience more than 2.3 million home injuries each year. Let's look at some of the leading causes:

- **Falls.** The National Center for Injury Control and Prevention reports that over one-third of people age 65+ suffer fall-related injuries. Some falls are the result of environmental hazards (an icy driveway, for example, or loose area rug), but others are due to the effects of aging. It's counterintuitive, we know, but balance is actually a "learned" behavior, requiring us to interpret and respond to information from our visual and vestibular (body positioning) systems. Age-related changes diminish perceptual acuity (so we don't process sensory feedback as well as we used to), while the part of the brain responsible for integrating and responding to this information deteriorates (so we're more likely to err in deciding how to move to regain our footing). On the positive side, research indicates that balance training can improve sensory integration skills much like a refresher driver's ed course improves driving. A physician can also refer you to a physical therapist for exercises to enhance your balance skills.

At some point you might need to replace outdoor stairs with railed, roofed ramps, or install a ramp or chair lift in the garage. Keep in mind that slope matters—and useable slopes are less steep than you'd think (a 1-inch rise for every foot of ramp is ideal). Don't forget flooring issues when designing an exterior ramp; choose durable, nonslip surfaces that can be cleared of snow or debris easily. Some ramps are made of open-mesh metal—good for drainage and fine for wheelchairs, but not great for walkers, cane tips, or shoe heels.

Handrails matter, too. These should be sturdy, and reachable from different heights. Make sure there's a stoop or porch area at the top of the ramp, wide enough to maneuver body, chair, and whatever one may be

- **Burns.** Less common than falls, burns are another significant cause of home injuries. Frying pan handles, cooktop burners, and spattering grease are obvious burn sources, but accidental hot water scaldings are also key culprits, especially for people with *neuropathy*—deterioration of the peripheral nervous system—which can diminish awareness of temperature, especially in the feet and lower legs. Antiscald devices should be installed in your plumbing system to moderate temperature extremes. (We had one installed a few years ago—they're not expensive, and since they're mounted near the water heater, they're not intrusive either.)

- **Poisoning.** Few of us would sip from a bottle without reading the label, but many of us take pills without reading the fine print about dosage recommendations, interactions, and contraindications. As more over-the-counter medications are available in extrastrength or extended-release formulas, it's easier than ever to take two tablets when one is actually the proper dosage. Dosages calculated for an active 45-year-old may be excessive for a 70-something adult whose ability to metabolize medication has slowed considerably over the years. As with all medications, vitamins, and supplements, ask your physician if a given over-the-counter preparation is right for you.

carrying in and out of the house (at least a 5 foot by 5 foot area is needed here). A raised level surface where one can place packages while locking or unlocking the door is also a plus.

BATHROOMS

You might not be surprised to learn that the most dangerous rooms in any home are the bathrooms and the kitchen. Why? Slips and falls. Many loss-of-balance accidents are the result of tiny misjudgments in distance while reaching for a towel from the tub or standing on a stepstool to inch an item from a high kitchen shelf. These tiny misjudgments can sometimes lead to serious falls followed by months of rehabilitation.

If you want to know whether your bathroom is truly accessible, stand or sit in the doorway and try to visualize how you would transfer from a wheelchair to the toilet safely using only one arm for leverage. Think about whether it would be possible to get in and out of the tub if your balance was impaired, as often happens when one develops a serious medical condition like diabetes or stroke. Try to brush your teeth using only your nondominant hand while remaining seated in front of the sink.

If your bathroom is like most, the need for strong, properly placed grab bars that can support your entire body weight will soon become apparent. You'll also appreciate raised toilet seats with arms to assist you as you get to your feet, shower stalls with sturdy seats and controls you can reach easily,

>> THE CERTIFIED AGING-IN-PLACE SPECIALIST

If you intend to have renovations done to make your home safer and more accessible, we strongly recommend that you employ a Certified Aging-in-Place Specialist (CAPS). To use this title, the contractor must undergo training in remodeling and renovation services, pass a test administered by the National Association of Home Builders (NAHB), and agree to abide by the Aging-in-Place Specialist Code of Ethics. (You can find a complete copy of the NAHB Code of Ethics, in downloadable form, on www.nahb.org; just enter "Code of Ethics" in the Search field.) As you'll see, the ethics code requires (among other things) that the Certified Aging-in-Place Specialist:

- Provide the most economical remodeling services possible.
- Protect the customer by using high-quality, low-maintenance materials.
- Stay informed regarding public policies and new regulations related to aging.
- Comply with rules and regulations regarding the health, safety, and welfare of the aging-in-place community.
- Respect clients' concerns and preferences without bias, ageism, or other forms of stereotyping.

showerheads that can be adjusted when you're seated or standing, and shelving you can use in the tub or stall.

Bathroom rugs may look homey, but they're accidents waiting to happen. If you can't give up these rugs entirely, make sure they're secured to the floor with carpet tape. You may be able to replace old flooring with easy-care, sustainable materials (like cork or bamboo) that are attractive without being slippery. Stick-on appliques render a slick shower floor safer (but avoid those rubber shower mats—they come loose at unexpected moments and actually increase the risk of a fall).

KITCHENS

Few kitchens were designed with wheelchairs in mind—especially wheelchairs that have extended leg rests or built-up arm supports. Find yourself chair-bound and you may discover that none of your kitchen tables or countertops is truly accessible—not one. Try to reach the kitchen sink faucet handles while sitting in a chair and you'll find that standard sinks are inaccessible too. The same goes for stoves: cooktops tend to be installed at heights too high to be reached safely from a wheelchair (especially the back burners). "Stacked" wall ovens and microwaves may be useless if you cannot stand and reach overhead (try to imagine how you'd maneuver a hot, heavy pot out of the oven if you could not stand or pivot).

The good news is, most kitchens are relatively roomy (at least compared to bathrooms), and they can usually be remodeled to suit your needs. Try to ensure that your kitchen has a number of flat surfaces at different heights, with ample open space below. Choose low ovens and side-by-side refrigerator/freezers so you'll have some accessible cooking and storage options. Side-opening oven doors are a better choice than conventional pull-down doors if you're wheelchair bound. Lever-style faucet handles or foot pedal controls are easier to use if manual dexterity is compromised, and antiscald devices (like those in your bathroom) prevent burns and the falls that sometimes result from flinching when we're surprised by too-hot water.

>> ON NOSY NEIGHBORS AND OTHER IMPORTANT THINGS

While police and security guards are important sources of protection and defense, long-term residents are often the keenest eyes and ears of any neighborhood, quick to spot subtle changes that an outsider might not notice. An observant resident may see a car unmoved in the driveway, lights not turned on at their usual time, or a newspaper not retrieved from the stoop, and realize right away that their neighbor isn't following his or her usual routines. (So don't be too hard on the neighborhood busybody who pokes her nose into everyone's business. Some day she might save your life.)

Such informal "security systems" are an important source of assistance, and a bit of preparation will go a long way toward ensuring that neighbors are looking out for you. You should:

- Make sure that one or two trusted neighbors have your phone numbers and email addresses, as well as those of your emergency contacts.

- Give at least one reliable neighbor a key, and any information necessary to turn off home alarms if they need to gain entry.

- Leave word with neighbors if you're having medical procedures done so someone will be able to look in on you (or keep an eye on the house) while you're away.

LIGHTING AND STORAGE

As we age, visual acuity diminishes and we require more light to see clearly. Consider installing overhead lights or adding lamps in high-traffic areas, and increasing the brightness of existing light fixtures (use the highest-wattage bulbs allowed for each). Motion sensitive lights in entries and hallways make walking around at night safer. Choose window treatments that allow you to use available natural light, and if remodeling is an option, you may want to add some accent windows that illuminate dark corners or entryways. Studies show that color can make a big difference in visibility as well: white and brightly colored surfaces make counters and workspaces more user-friendly.

If you look closely at the storage areas in your home, you'll realize that most were designed to take advantage of inaccessible space. Many kitchen cabinets are high overhead, while bathroom storage units tend to be hidden under sinks. Oftentimes storage areas are tucked under stairways, or near the ceiling in the laundry room.

Clearly, these storage options were designed with the able-bodied in mind—you have to be able to stand, reach, bend, or kneel to get at them. Consider installing "pullout" ("lazy Susan") style shelving so you can bring the back of the drawer or closet to you. Reacher devices—metal poles with grasping implements at one end—can be a great help, and they're available at most hardware stores, but remember that an item at the end of a 2-foot-long pole will seem heavier and clumsier than the same item held in your hand.

Weather Fair and Foul

Four years living in Buffalo, New York, taught us something: climate considerations are important where safe living is concerned. While graduate students attending SUNY at Buffalo in the early 1980s, we—like everyone else—struggled to get around during those difficult western New York winters. Shoveling a parking space or driveway to free a snow-buried car was tiring when we were in our 20s. Now that we're both in our 50s, it's hard to imagine coping with such challenging conditions year in, year out.

There's no doubt about it: your physical health and emotional well-being are impacted by the weather. You cannot eliminate weather-related issues, of course—every place has its problems. And depending where you live, you may have to prepare for potentially serious events like hurricanes, tornadoes, floods, or earthquakes. Even as we write this chapter, drought-fueled wildfires are approaching Colorado Springs; several dozen homes have already been destroyed. (Update: It's now four months later, we're doing final edits on this chapter, and we're in the midst of recovering from Hurricane Sandy, which devastated our region five days ago. Weather emergencies are more common than one might think.)

Regardless of whether your area experiences these sorts of challenges, it's wise to develop a game plan for the most likely weather-related emergencies, whatever they may be. You might never need to use your escape route, but if you do, you'll be glad you had it planned ahead of time.

Some home safety issues are related to the physical layout of your home (such as too-steep stairs). But sometimes home safety issues have nothing to do with the space itself—they come from the person. Memory is among the most important requirements for being able to function independently and age in place; in the next section we look at how problems in memory can impact home safety.

- First aid kit
- At least a week's supply of essential medications
- Multipurpose knife tool and can/bottle opener
- A set of eating utensils in a ziplock bag
- Pen and small notebook
- Cash (credit cards don't work in some emergency situations)
- Copies of key identification documents (passport, driver's license, Medicare card)
- Important information about bank accounts, current prescriptions, etc.
- High-nutrient snacks (like energy bars)
- A map of the area

As you might imagine, such a bag could get heavy quickly as you think of other things you'd want with you if you had to relocate in a hurry. The importance of packing light must be weighed against that of inclusiveness (you can't bring everything, so be selective). Once it's packed, store the bag where you can access it easily. And remember to check it at least once every six months so you can update or replace contents as needed.

When Memory Fades: Strategies to Prolong Aging in Place

Everyone has moments of failing memory—misplaced keys, missed appointments, misremembered names. When are these events just blips on the radar, and when do they represent a more serious problem? More than four million adults in the United States suffer from Alzheimer's disease—about one of every seventy people—and though memory loss due to Alzheimer's disease or some other form of dementia does not preclude aging in place, it does require some additional accommodation.

Keep in mind that the memory failures we often find most troubling (forgetting what month it is, being unable to recall our grandchildren's names) are not necessarily those that create the greatest problems in living. Thinking that it's still March when it's actually April is embarrassing—but no one has ever entered a nursing home because they misestimated the date. The more serious memory problems—the ones that may potentially require a higher level of care—are those that put the person or others at risk: forgetting to turn off the stove when you're done cooking dinner, for example, or heading down the block for the newspaper wearing only slippers and a nightshirt.

DISTINGUISHING NORMAL MEMORY LOSS FROM A MORE SERIOUS PROBLEM

To determine whether memory problems warrant formal evaluation by a physician, look for three things:

- **A pattern rather than a single incident.** Occasional "senior moments" happen to everyone, especially when we're tired, stressed, anxious, or ill. Everybody draws a blank once in a while, but if you've forgotten a series of important dates, or friends have begun to call ahead of time to remind you to show up for appointments, the behavior is now part of a pattern, and could be an early sign of memory loss.

- **Not remembering how familiar things work.** Misplacing one's keys is not a sign of dementia. Holding keys in one's hand and not knowing what they are used for might well be. To the degree that memory problems involve an inability to recall how things work, and what they are used for, the likelihood of a more serious problem increases. (Of course this only holds for familiar items—trouble figuring out how to use your new tablet or smart phone doesn't count.)

- **Memory failings accompanied by language difficulties.** Forgetting a name every once in a while isn't unusual, but if your speech becomes peppered with substitute words ("that thingy" or "the whatchamacallit"), you may have a problem. Inability to express yourself concisely— rambling conversation—is also a troubling sign (so if friends start urging you to get to the point, consider that a red flag). Repetitiveness can be a red flag as well: if people tell you you're asking the same question over and over, it's time to take action.

>> WHEN EXTRA HELP IS NEEDED: COMMON SIGNS OF FUNCTIONAL DECLINE

Here are the most common signs of cognitive decline and memory loss that suggest independent living may be difficult without extra help; if you or your partner show more than one or two of these signs, a higher level of care (like assisted living) may be needed. Be on the lookout for:

- Problems with storing or preparing food (for example, spoiled milk, burned or undercooked meat, charred or blackened pots and pans)
- Trouble completing tasks (for example, discovering that you left your clothes in the washing machine overnight, having forgotten to put them in the dryer)
- Difficulty communicating (for example, rambling conversation, inability to find words to express a thought), or repetitive questioning (along with an inability to remember the other person's response)
- Difficulty paying bills (for example, problems deciphering the bills, doing the math, or writing the checks), or keeping track of bank accounts (for example, bouncing checks)
- Persistent confusion about the date, day of week, or time of day
- Forgetting how to use familiar implements (like a key) or perform simple tasks (like opening a bottle of pills)
- Reports from friends and neighbors of strange behavior
- Getting lost—especially if you can't find your way home from a familiar place
- Repeatedly forgetting to take your medication

CHARACTERISTICS OF EARLY-STAGE MEMORY LOSS

Most people experiencing the early signs of dementia are aware that something is wrong, and they begin searching for information to figure out what's going on. Not surprisingly, many people consult their physician, seeking tests and treatments. Tests can be helpful, but keep in mind that while some dementing conditions have obvious physical substrates (like signs of stroke or brain atrophy), many do not. This is one area of medicine where structure does not always mirror function: some people with extensive brain atrophy are virtually helpless, while others with very similar patterns function normally. The most accurate information regarding functional capacity—one's ability to independently carry out the activities of daily living—will come not from brain images but from neuropsychological tests that assess a broad array of cognitive skills.

Ironically, these neuropsychological tests, while highly accurate, are of limited use at the earliest stages because the results tend to confirm what you already know—you *might* have a problem which bears watching. The good news is, having now established your baseline level of cognitive functioning, periodic retesting can yield very useful data, helping identify areas of loss and allowing your physician to generate a reasonably accurate prediction of how (and how rapidly) things will progress.

A few issues to keep in mind as you make decisions at this stage:

- **Losses may not be reflected in all—or even most—areas.** While some forms of dementia cause across-the-board deterioration, many dementias yield "patchy" deficits—some skills are essentially untouched while others are ravaged (which is why you sometimes encounter a person who can hold an informed conversation about global economic issues yet not remember what day it is). Psychological testing often yields useful predictions about which functions are likely to be preserved, and which ones lost—information that is very helpful in planning ahead.

- **Let reason—not emotion—rule.** Panic is not a helpful response to the possibility of dementia, though it's certainly understandable. If you sense that you're having memory problems, the first question you may want to ask yourself is "What would I do differently if I knew for sure that I have dementia?" For many people, the answer involves shifting priorities and doing some things that they'd been putting off—taking that trip to Hawaii, for example, or spending more time with the grandchildren. Many people use this opportunity to formalize future plans, like writing a will or establishing advance directives.

(We discussed the basics of wills, advance directives, powers of attorney, and other important legal matters in chapter 1.)

- **Most decisions involve tradeoffs.** Ticking off the items on one's "bucket list" may seem reasonable when faced with the possibility of dementia—why not do things while you can still enjoy them? That sort of thinking is fine, but keep in mind that for many of us such dreams were deferred for a reason: finite resources. Liquidating your 401(k) or reverse-mortgaging the house to fund a lavish dream vacation may be predicated on the assumption that time is fleeting, but dementia is a progressive disease, not altogether predictable, and often slower than you'd think. Many people with dementia live happily and safely in their own homes during the early and middle stages of the illness, as long as they can afford appropriate accommodations (like in-home care). Needless to say, these accommodations tend to be expensive, so a round-the-world cruise today may diminish your nest egg to the point that you'd have to enter a nursing home sooner rather than later. The bottom line: Weigh the relative value of "once in a lifetime" opportunities against prolonging the lifestyle you've grown to love. There's no right answer here; it's an individual decision.

AGING IN PLACE ACCOMMODATIONS FOR LIMITED OR FAILING MEMORY

Once you've determined that additional support is needed, there are things you can do. These are among the most important:

- **Implementing orienting cues.** *Orienting cues* are sources of information that tell you where you are and what you should be doing. A familiar environment, in and of itself, is an invaluable orienting cue, and a key resource for successful aging in place ("If it's 7 a.m. and I'm standing in the kitchen, it's time to make the coffee"). Clocks and calendars are among our most basic—and most helpful—orienting cues: even in late stages of dementia, when many other skills have deteriorated, people still look to clocks and calendars to orient themselves, and decide what tasks should come next. TV can help too: every cable company offers at least one 24/7 news channel that provides frequent reminders of date and time. The same electronic or paper datebooks and calendars that kept you organized at work can keep you on schedule for appointments, meetings, and other events today. And literal bells and whistles are available to prompt certain tasks: you can purchase pillboxes that sound an alert when it's time to take your medication, or install software on your computer (or an app on your smart phone) that will remind you of just about anything—you decide.

- **Maintaining the environment to reduce risk.** A well-maintained house is the best defense against many risks related to memory loss. In early dementia, one's ability to respond rapidly to unexpected problems deteriorates (so panic at the sound of a smoke alarm may lead to a fall down the stairs rather than appropriate corrective action). Prevention is the strategy of choice here, so repair or replace those appliances and fixtures that you've meant to get around to fixing. Replace old fire extinguishers, and be sure you know how to use the new ones. Make sure fire and smoke alarms, carbon monoxide detectors, and burglar alarms are in good working order, and that you know how to activate and deactivate them reliably. Consider investing in a personal emergency response system (PERS) so you can summon help quickly (we discuss these response systems on page 102).

- **Obtaining in-home care.** The ideal accommodation for diminished memory is having somebody there to help, and more often than not spouses or partners provide this sort of support early on in the process. Sometimes two members of a couple have different needs and each can assist the other, and studies show that those willing to take on new roles and responsibilities may be able to extend their joint independence significantly (for example, the healthier partner takes the wheel as the less healthy partner's driving abilities wane). When memory loss becomes too great for the healthier partner to handle, it's important to be realistic as well: in-home care can prolong aging in place, and improve your quality of life immeasurably (we discussed in-home care options in chapter 2). If you feel selfish spending money on in-home care because of failing memory, keep in mind that regardless of who is the "identified patient," both partners will benefit. In-home care provides the healthier person an opportunity to rest, recharge his or her batteries, run errands, and attend to various personal matters. In this respect, in-home care not only helps keep the person with memory problems safe and comfortable, it represents an important source of support for the healthier partner as well.

>> WARNING SIGNS OF A DISHONEST CONTRACTOR

It's no secret that crooks see retirees as easy targets. Older adults are particularly vulnerable to financial scammers, crooked contractors, and other fly-by-night salespeople. It's not always possible to distinguish an honest, earnest contractor from a manipulative, dishonest scammer, but here are some warning signs to look for. If any of these occur, just say no:

- The sales contact was initiated by the contractor, not by you.
- You're pressured to sign papers right then and there—you're told the deal will no longer be available if you delay.
- The salesperson has a fancy title (like Senior Housing Specialist or Eldercare Renovation Expert) that you've never heard before—and they emphasize that title throughout the sales pitch.
- The contractor hesitates or makes excuses when you ask for references from satisfied customers.
- You are asked for a large down payment or substantial amount of money up front. (Thirty percent or so is standard for most contractors, and no money changes hands until the contract is signed.)
- It sounds too good to be true. (If it sounds that way, it probably is.)

As you can see, some aspects of making your home safer and more accessible are simple, and can be accomplished fairly easily with a trip to the hardware store. Other changes require more extensive planning, and greater cost. In the end, though, when you consider the benefit of improving home safety—making your personal space "livable" for a lifetime— even the major projects begin to seem more feasible. It's worth it: you'll be protecting yourself in ways that really count.

CHAPTER 4

Getting Around

Mobility means autonomy. With it you can manage your home, shop on your own, take advantage of entertainment and recreational opportunities, and access needed services (like the bank and the doctor). If mobility is compromised, your ability to carry out ADLs will be limited, and the likelihood of successful aging in place diminishes.

The National Rehabilitation Information Center estimates that approximately twenty-five million Americans have significant mobility impairment (difficulty walking, getting into or out of vehicles, or navigating physical spaces without extensive assistance). Leading causes include arthritis, stroke, balance and coordination problems, muscle weakness (sometimes resulting from falls and other injuries), and neurological disorders (like Parkinson's disease). Many of these problems can be improved with medical treatment or physical therapy, but some are chronic conditions that must be managed and accommodated.

Access is a key component of the AOS model, and crucial for a happy, healthy retirement, so as you plan, you should consider how you would manage if you could no longer get around on your own. Think about how you would get from place to place if at some point you can't drive, or if you require a wheelchair, walker, or other assistive device. This is one area of planning in which it is wise to make no assumptions: check out transportation options *before* you choose a place to live, and remember to keep yourself updated on any changes that occur (oftentimes public transit schedules are trimmed when budgets get tight, as happened in our area, Nassau County, New York, following the 2008 financial crisis).

Good health usually means good mobility, but the environment matters, too. Even the healthiest person can't get where they need to if sidewalks are in disrepair, the neighborhood is unsafe, or traffic patterns make crossing the street impossible. In this chapter, we discuss the basics of getting around: neighborhood walkability (and how to assess it), driving options (including public and subsidized transportation), and legal issues related to mobility and access.

The Advantages of Walkability

Ideally, your home is situated so that every essential service can be accessed on foot (though for the most part this level of convenience is only available in urban areas and smaller towns—suburbs tend to be among the least "walkable" locales of all). The list of accessible "essentials" varies from person to person, but there are some goods and services nearly everyone must have. (Grocery stores, pharmacies, banks, post offices, hairdressers, doctors' offices, dry cleaners, libraries, and houses of worship are some of the more crucial sites.) Beyond access, walkability brings other advantages that contribute to a successful retirement. Three stand out:

> Good health usually means good mobility, but the environment matters, too. Even the healthiest person can't get where they need to if sidewalks are in disrepair, the neighborhood is unsafe, or traffic patterns make crossing the street impossible.

- **Exercise and recreation.** Walking is one of the most pleasant forms of exercise, and because it is low impact, it's an ideal way to stay fit through your 70s and beyond. Walking enhances lung function, muscle strength, endurance, stamina, and balance. It can also be a great diet aid—numerous studies have shown that people who live in more walkable areas weigh less on average than their car-dependent counterparts. If you feel the need for additional exercise options, you'll also want to determine if your home is within walking distance of local parks, golf courses, pools, gyms, skating rinks, and other recreational venues. Movies, theaters, concert halls, sports arenas, senior centers, and schools may also be important to you—and if you don't have to worry about the costs and hassles of transportation or parking, you'll be more likely to take advantage of these opportunities.

- **Social contact.** Researchers have found that with each hour spent commuting, one's social network shrinks a bit. Conversely, the more you walk in your neighborhood, the greater the likelihood you'll interact with those who live near you. A truly walkable area allows access for people of all ages, resulting in a mix of adults and children, parents and grandparents. A walkable locale helps create a true neighborhood—a place to connect, interact, and share news, good and bad.

- **Increased safety.** Foot traffic tends to diminish crime, as it provides extra eyes and ears familiar with the setting—a collective of neighbors who'll notice immediately if something seems odd or out of place. The presence of passersby also increases the likelihood that someone will report small problems before they become major issues. The rough road surface gets patched before it turns into a giant pothole; minor acts of mischief are brought to police attention before they escalate into expensive acts of vandalism. (An additional advantage: studies indicate that your home's value rises as the neighborhood becomes more walkable.)

Evaluating Walkability

The only way to determine the walkability of a neighborhood is to boot up and head out there—nothing beats first-hand experience. On page 216 we've provided a Walkability Checklist, which you can use to assess various features of your neighborhood, how easy it will be to get around, and what sorts of challenges you're likely to encounter along the way. You can also use the checklist to compare different neighborhoods and judge which are easiest to navigate on foot; this information can be useful if you're deciding among possible locations to retire. Various Internet sites are also available that allow you to compare the walkability of different locales. (We've included some in our resource list, which begins on page 223.)

As you can see from our checklist, there are literally dozens of issues to consider when evaluating neighborhood walkability. Most fall into three categories—distances, surfaces and crossings, and traffic.

>> ROLLABILITY

We had been encouraging some wheelchair-bound folks to use the lovely patio that backed a local nursing facility, and were puzzled by their reluctance. One day we accompanied a chair-bound friend outside, and then we understood why nobody used the space. The doors were heavy, not equipped with an automatic opening device, and virtually impossible to move through in a wheelchair. The flagstones outside were uneven, snagging the wheels repeatedly and leaving our friend in danger of tipping. Our every move was clearly visible from the office staff's first floor windows, destroying any illusion of privacy (though this latter problem actually proved helpful when we got stuck on the threshold while attempting reentry and needed to be rescued).

If you or a loved one is wheelchair-bound, evaluating walkability means evaluating rollability. Some additional challenges that arise:

- Allowing extra time to get across the street (and be sure to test out crossings during busy, high-traffic times as well as quieter, less busy ones)

- Paying particular attention to curb transitions (sidewalk to street and street to sidewalk)

- Finding out which businesses and restaurants are—and are not— wheelchair accessible

- Looking for narrow areas on sidewalks that might hinder rollability (these may be caused by obstacles like bike racks, outdoor dining areas, and sidewalk vendors)

- Evaluating rollability during inclement weather conditions (ice, rain, snow) as well as pleasant ones

DISTANCES

Local Chambers of Commerce are notorious for providing unrealistic, overly optimistic figures regarding the accessibility of various neighborhoods, so ignore these and focus on actual (physical) distance. Be sure to take into account changes in elevation; hills can be difficult to navigate (and walking downhill is sometimes harder than walking uphill). A mile-long trek to the post office doesn't sound bad, but as you age your endurance may diminish, making a once-walkable distance impractical, especially when it's hot out, or the weather is inclement. After a few inches of snow, or in torrential rain, even a three-block walk could render grocery shopping nearly impossible.

SURFACES AND CROSSINGS

Maps can be deceiving; don't assume that sidewalks are available and in good shape. In many suburban and rural areas, sidewalks are optional, which can result in "broken field walking" as you try to get from one place to another. Even in those areas where sidewalks are the norm, their actual condition may vary substantially. Uneven pavement isn't a minor nuisance—it can be a major obstacle if you're trying to manage a grocery cart and an umbrella on a wet and windy day. And if homeowners pay little attention to clearing ice and snow from the sidewalk, your route may be useless—literally impassable—during much of the winter. (One of our personal peeves: those who only clear a narrow shovel-width path down the center of the sidewalk—thanks a lot!)

Crossings should be assessed carefully. Roads cannot be navigated safely without clearly marked crosswalks and traffic signals that allow adequate time to get across. Parking patterns also make a difference: to be safe, you must be able to see—and be seen by—drivers in all traffic lanes; if you're hidden by a line of tightly parked (or double-parked) vehicles, drivers might not have adequate time to react when you enter the crosswalk. Also check for landscaping that obscures the view—decorative bushes, low-hanging tree branches, and privacy fencing can render a corner crossing hazardous.

TRAFFIC

Sheer volume of vehicle traffic should also be considered when assessing walkability—even in pedestrian-friendly cities, the incidence of vehicle-pedestrian accidents is greater in high-traffic than low-traffic areas. While cars and trucks are the most likely culprits, don't minimize the hazard of bicycles, skateboards, and other wheelies. Oftentimes these quasi-pedestrians share the walking space nicely, but some skateboarders and bikers can be reckless, and collisions are not unheard-of. Keep in mind that an actual collision need not occur for you to be put in jeopardy: sometimes a pedestrian, startled by an unexpected bicycle whizzing by, takes a misstep, stumbles, and falls.

Driving in Place

For many people, mobility means driving. Nothing gives you the freedom to go where you want quite like having your own vehicle (which is probably why every teenager in history perfected their nagging skills by bugging parents about getting a car). Driving has tremendous symbolic importance as well: many older adults continue to drive long after they've given up other physical pursuits, so driving tends to be the last bastion of true independence. Nowadays many destinations are designed to be accessible only by car (think suburban grocery stores and shopping malls). Lacking wheels, you literally can't get there from here.

SMART CARS

If you're currently of retirement age, you probably remember cars that ran on leaded gasoline, lacked power steering and power brakes, and didn't always include seatbelts (besides, who used those things back then?). Every car had ashtrays and cigarette lighters, but air conditioning was an expensive luxury. A certain degree of physical strength was needed to park cleanly, and to hold the wheel steady over rough road surfaces.

Technological improvements have made driving easier, and more vision friendly as well: advanced optics and cameras can now capture every inch of your surrounding area (including "blind spots"), and some vehicles literally park themselves or stop quickly when they sense an unexpected barrier. While technological advances cannot replace safe driving, vehicles are increasingly designed to protect us from ourselves. Keep in mind that all those bells and whistles don't come cheap—just because technology exists doesn't mean it's universally available or financially feasible for everyone. Typically, "smart" cars with cutting-edge innovations tend to run about $5,000 to $8,000 more than similar models with fewer sophisticated electronics, but like many new technologies, smart car prices are slowly beginning to moderate as demand increases and production costs decline. Still, if you can afford some of these extras, you may want to make the investment so you'll have them in place as your needs increase.

>> DRUGGED DRIVING

Many drivers who would be aghast at the thought of driving under the influence of alcohol think nothing of getting behind the wheel after swallowing prescription pills. Fact is, many commonly prescribed drugs (and many over-the-counter medications as well) alter perception, slow reaction time, and impair driving ability.

Don't assume that your driving skill is unaffected by your medication regimen. Next time you have a checkup, ask your doctor whether your medications could affect your driving, and if so take that into account when making driving decisions. If you're unsure, have someone you trust—someone who knows you well enough to give an honest, uncensored opinion—come along and let you know whether they feel safe riding with you.

SAFE DRIVING PROGRAMS

The stereotype of the confused senior blissfully driving down the sidewalk winging innocent pedestrians is just that—a stereotype—but make no mistake: such incidents have occurred, and older drivers are definitely a high-risk group. National Highway Traffic Safety Administration data indicate that although people age 70+ make up about 9 percent of the population, they account for 14 percent of all traffic fatalities and 17 percent of pedestrian fatalities. The fatality rate for drivers 85 and over is nine times as high as the rate for drivers 25 through 69 years old. There's no denying the fact that we see less well and react less quickly as we age.

The good news is, many skills can be improved with coaching, and research has shown that driving performance improves considerably following a brief refresher course that reviews best practices and gives advice on how to deal with the perceptual and functional declines that come with age. AAA and AARP are among the organizations that sponsor such programs, and many insurance companies offer discounts on policy fees to drivers who attend these classes (we're saving 10 percent on our premiums because we both completed such a class last year). Some people avoid taking safe driving programs, fearing that the programs are actually intended to police those whose skills may be deteriorating. But most folks who have taken refresher driving courses find that they pick up some useful pointers along the way (we sure did).

> Research has shown that driving performance improves considerably following a brief refresher course that reviews best practices and gives advice on how to deal with the perceptual and functional declines that come with age.

Being Realistic: When Not to Drive

We understand that driving is important, which is why people are reluctant to give it up. Still, when driving becomes unsafe, we urge you to stop. The consequences of denying driving problems can be catastrophic: in 2003, 86-year-old Russell Weller became confused and drove three blocks through a crowded farmers' market in Santa Monica, California, killing nine people and injuring more than fifty others.

Here are four warning signs that suggest you can no longer drive safely:

- **Vision problems.** If you can't see clearly, you shouldn't drive. Enough said.
- **You're out of practice.** Many people continue to hold onto their driver's licenses even though they haven't used them in decades—

understandable because a driver's license is one of the most widely accepted forms of identification. Keeping your license makes sense, but if you haven't driven in many years, don't assume you can start up the engine and pick up where you left off.

- **Frequent near misses.** Are you finding that the number of times you've had to swerve or stop short to avoid an accident has increased lately? If so, it's a sign that you are no longer seeing well enough or reacting quickly enough to be a safe driver.

- **Other drivers letting you know.** We live on Long Island, where honking is a sign of affection. Everyone annoys another driver every once in a while, but if the frequency of horn blasts and hand gestures aimed in your direction has increased lately, pay attention. Your fellow drivers are telling you something.

PUBLIC TRANSPORTATION

There comes a point in the life of many retirees where opting to stop driving is the smart thing to do. If your vision is impaired or your reactions are slowed to the point that it's no longer safe to pilot a vehicle, do the right thing—don't get behind the wheel. Recent estimates indicate that over 20 percent of people over 65 no longer drive, making alternate forms of transportation essential.

Sadly, a 2005 survey by AARP's Public Policy Institute found that fewer than half of those over 65 live within reasonable walking distance of public transportation (which is why you need to check on this ahead of time, before you decide where to plant your retirement roots). Just as you should evaluate neighborhood walkability by venturing out on foot, the only way to evaluate the usefulness of public transportation is to try it out yourself. Your doctor's office might indeed be accessible by bus, but if it takes three transfers and ninety minutes to get there, this is not really a viable long-term solution. You can obtain information regarding public transportation options in your area by contacting your local town or county government website, or Google using the search term "Public Transportation [your town or county name here]" (for example, "Public Transportation Cincinnati" or "Public Transportation Dutchess County").

SUBSIDIZED TRANSPORTATION

Most areas provide subsidized handicapped-accessible transportation for people with physical disabilities and limited incomes. Paratransit services, supplemental transportation programs (STPs), and human services transportation systems all fall into this category. Application fees for membership are usually minimal (sometimes free), and the per-ride cost is considerably less than standard taxi fare or ambulette charges. (Note: Ambulettes are specially equipped vehicles—usually vans—designed to transport people seated in wheelchairs). Some paratransit services provide transport only to medical appointments, while others will take you to any destination within their geographic area (these geographic limits are often county based because the services tend to be county funded). You can obtain information regarding paratransit services in your area by contacting your local Agency on Aging, or Google using the search term "Paratransit [your town or county name here]" (for example, "Paratransit Memphis" or "Paratransit Blaine County").

Keep in mind that multiple riders are included in most subsidized trips, and the company determines the route. Reservations are generally required at least a day in advance (sometimes earlier around high-traffic times such as holidays), and if the day's roster is full, you're out of luck. Pickup times are often given in half-hour windows to allow for traffic and other delays. Liability considerations may require that riders be ready "at curbside" when they pull up. (Drivers are not permitted to help you exit a building or get up or down stairs, and can offer only minimal assistance as you board or exit the vehicle.) Many services allow a helper to ride with you for free, as long as you tell them in advance so they can plan space accordingly.

Although the service dispatcher designs the route, the driver has final say based on traffic conditions and other considerations. Those who use these services regularly usually have some harrowing tales of mile-long journeys that took three hours to complete. Drivers are allowed to stop no

>> CAR CLUBS AND CAR POOLS

Cars cost way more than that number on the sticker. There's the price of the car (or the annual lease), fees to register and inspect it, and the costs of insurance, maintenance, fuel, and parking. You have control over some of these factors (you can buy a cheaper car or opt for less expensive insurance), but most of the costs that make owning or leasing a car an expensive proposition are out of your hands (insurance premiums increase—there's nothing you can do about it).

If you want to cut costs, informal car pools may serve your needs well. Banding together with neighbors to pool resources for a day of shopping can save fuel, provide extra hands for carrying packages, and offer company and companionship (plus safety in numbers). If you don't have a car but would like to begin a carpool network with friends or neighbors, a good place to start is to offer to pay for gas and/or a lunch out on the town on shopping day. Don't underestimate the value of simply taking the lead on this: oftentimes arrangements that benefit lots of people don't happen simply because no one bothered to take the initiative. Becoming the organizer is a great way to be included, even if you don't have wheels (or don't drive).

more than ten or fifteen minutes at any given site, so if you're not there at the scheduled time they go on without you. This can be rather a headache if you're at a doctor's appointment and your doctor is running late, but drivers will generally swing back to get you if they miss you on the first try.

Another subsidized transportation option involves senior centers, which sometimes offer limited transportation to and from members' homes, and have regularly scheduled trips to grocery stores, malls, and other popular destinations. Many assisted living facilities, senior communities, and NORCs have similar arrangements. The door-to-door nature of these services makes them very convenient, but like most subsidized services, these are usually dependent on funding sources beyond the control of

If you live in a major city and only need a car occasionally, you may want to consider a car sharing club. You pay a fee to get a passcard that gives you access to vehicles stored around town; when you need a car, you call or email the company, which directs you to the nearest one that's available. The passcard unlocks the vehicle, and you drive as you like then return the car to a preset location. You rent by the hour or by the day, and the rental cost includes insurance. You can request the size and type of vehicle you need; some fleets even have vehicles with hand-operated controls to accommodate disabled drivers. Most programs include emergency roadside assistance if you break down. Zipcar and City Car Share are two popular services; rentals currently start around $12 per hour (visit their websites, www.zipcar.com and www.carsharing.net, for more information).

Though they have many advantages, car sharing clubs aren't perfect: like any rental car service, reservation glitches are not unknown, and late returns often result in steep penalties. There are restrictions on who may drive, and base costs are augmented by fees and taxes that can render the bottom line more costly. There's a mileage allowance, with extra charges if you go further, so you need to know ahead of time how far you plan to go. Still, despite these restrictions and potential glitches, if you only need a car once in a while, car sharing may be a viable option.

the organizations and people who run them. Some nonprofits with senior programs offer transportation to medical appointments (and elsewhere); these are usually staffed by volunteer drivers who enjoy working with older adults. Such programs are subsidized by the nonprofit organization and many (not all) are free for those who meet eligibility criteria (these vary from program to program).

When Access Is Denied

Originally enacted in 1990, the Americans with Disabilities Act (ADA) "prohibits discrimination and ensures equal opportunities and access for persons with disabilities." As a result, buses and trains are now designed with physically challenged people in mind. Steps have been replaced with curb-height entrance ramps, aisles are wider, grab bars and supports are well-placed, and wheelchair bays are more plentiful. Bus stops have appropriate curb cuts and seating options, and accessible shelter.

Things are moving forward, but not as quickly as one might hope. Most buses and trains were designed to last a long time, so many older (pre-ADA) vehicles are still in use, to be replaced gradually as they wear out. Ditto for pre-ADA buildings: many must be retrofitted to conform to ADA accessibility regulations, but the process will take some time. Even though airports are technically accessible, byzantine handicapped access routes sometimes render timely connections between flights nearly impossible. (It's best to plan ahead—and call ahead—if you have to make a tight connection.)

The bottom line: Eventually we'll get there, but more than twenty years after the law was first passed, ADA remains a work in progress.

EXCEPTIONS TO ADA

Public transportation services that receive federal and state funding must be accessible—no exceptions, no excuses. Small, privately owned businesses aren't subject to the same standards because such a requirement could pose "undue hardship" on individual business owners and force many to close up shop. Complicating matters, the boundaries between public

>> GOLF CARS, ELECTRIC SCOOTERS, AND OTHER NON-CAR OPTIONS

Many retirees—especially those in planned communities—are using golf cars and scooters to get around these days, and such modes of transportation are indeed very convenient. But use caution when driving these vehicles—think of them as if they were cars, and use the same discretion you would if you were getting behind the wheel of a Buick. Because of their modest size and speed, it's tempting to think that golf cars, scooters, and other "non-car" options carry little risk of injury, but that's not the case. Numerous fatal and nonfatal accidents involving these vehicles have occurred, both on and off-road, and the frequency of serious golf car and scooter mishaps has increased in recent years.

Technically classified as "neighborhood electric vehicles" (NEVs) or "low-speed vehicles" (LSVs), golf cars and other non-car methods for getting around are regulated by the National Highway Traffic Safety Administration (NHTSA) and subject to some fairly stringent rules and regulations. Like a regular car (or boat), you are not permitted to drive an NEV when under the influence of alcohol or drugs. In fact, comedian Bill Murray was pulled over in 2007 for driving a golf car while under the influence (yes, we see the irony here).

The physical structure and design of NEVs are also tightly regulated. Among other things, they must:

- Have a maximum speed of 35 miles per hour
- Be equipped with headlights, taillights, and turn signals
- Have interior and exterior rear- and sideview mirrors
- Have a seat belt at each seat (four seats maximum)
- Have a vehicle identification number clearly visible

Keep in mind that this is only a partial list of NEV regulations and requirements; each state (and many local communities) have their own NEV laws as well. You can learn more about safe operation of NEVs on the NHTSA website (go to www.nhtsa.gov and search using the terms *NEV* or *LSV*).

and private aren't always clear; many public transportation services operate out of private spaces, or lease equipment from privately owned companies. As a result, you might encounter some practical challenges where public and private connect (for example, an accessible bus or train may have stops scheduled at inaccessible locations).

Technical glitches can also complicate otherwise easy trips. We've encountered that fairly often when riding the Washington, DC, Metro: elevator outages require riders unable to use the stairs or escalators to remain on the train for extra stops then catch a free Metro-owned van back to the stop they really wanted. Needless to say, these issues are politically and legally complex, but from the perspective of the passenger trying to get somewhere, they're just frustrating.

>> UNFAIR FARES

It's illegal, but we've still heard a number of people complain bitterly of extra baggage fees added to taxi fares when they need to have walkers, braces, or other assistive equipment stored in the trunk. Not surprisingly, most people paid when asked, not wanting to make a fuss (or have their stuff held hostage by the driver). Those who did refuse often encountered some significant unpleasantness.

You should know that such fees are illegal, and even if you feel as though you must pay to de-escalate the situation and avoid a confrontation, you can still report the violation to your local better business bureau or taxi commission when you're home and your ride is over.

PLANNING AHEAD WHEN ACCESS IS UNCERTAIN

Retirees have managed to survive and thrive in rural and hard-to-access areas for many years, so limited public transportation need not be a complete deal-breaker when you're deciding where to age in place. If your locale has some public transit, try it out—take the bus to the grocery store, or the subway to your next doctor's appointment. You may be pleasantly surprised, and if not, at least you'll know that option is off the table.

Regardless of how good the current public transportation system is, you'd be wise to ponder possible strategies and solutions in advance, in case transportation funding is cut. Ask yourself: Could your NORC or faith group chip in to fund an accessible van if needed, along with some driver time each week? Can you develop a roster of volunteers willing to donate their driving skills if you provide the wheels and gas? Could you identify private funding sources to support a shared ride program that meets your needs? If the answer to all these questions is no, you'll be completely dependent on the current system to get around.

PLAYING POLITICS

To the surprise of those who live in urban areas, many rural regions have no public transportation whatsoever, and few private options. When we moved to Gettysburg, Pennsylvania, back in 1986, we were surprised to discover that there was no taxi service in the area—none. Nor was there in-town bus service. Residents who didn't drive were stuck—and when Greyhound eliminated their Gettysburg stop in the mid-1990s, nondrivers were literally unable to leave town. It's something to think about if you're considering a move to a rural area.

Not surprisingly, area agencies on aging in these regions tend to devote considerable lobbying effort to obtaining subsidized transportation options for older residents. The AARP and the National Center on Senior Transportation (of the National Association of Area Agencies on Aging) both offer a wealth of information on model programs, community initiatives, and grants available to develop affordable transportation options in underserved rural locales. (Check out their websites—they're in our resource list. See page 223.)

These organizations also offer political action suggestions for those in urban areas, where lobbying efforts are directed toward ensuring that new public transit hubs are built near affordable housing developments. This movement has a name—it's called Transit Oriented Development (TOD)—and it can greatly enhance the likelihood of successful aging in place for those who live in underserved urban areas. Lobbying efforts can also be directed toward enhancing community walkability and traffic safety through zoning law changes, public works programs, and building initiatives. Retirees are well organized, and have a strong voter voice, but only if they—and you—use it.

There you have it: Being able to get where you need to go is an essential component of independent living, and crucial for aging in place, so be certain that your retirement locale has the physical layout and transportation infrastructure that will enable you to get around, even if your mobility declines and you need some additional assistance. Check out the area and investigate transportation options up front, and as you do, have in mind where you'll need to go, both now and in the future.

>> TOURS AND GETAWAYS

The idea of "senior tours" can send shudders down the sophisticated traveler's spine, conjuring as it does images of an unwieldy bus filled with camera-laden folks clamoring to get a shot of the schlockiest tourist traps in town. That was then, this is now: as the boomer population has grown, the market for senior tours has increased accordingly. Things have changed—it's time to let go of outmoded stereotypes.

Modern tours for retirement-age people offer a broad range of options—learning adventures for those who want in-depth exposure to a particular topic (like art or wine tasting), small groups offering up-close-and-personal encounters with formerly inaccessible areas, groups specifically aimed at solo travelers seeking same-age company, and family-friendly experiences suitable for sharing with children and grandchildren. Many of these tours are sponsored by colleges and universities, by religious groups (like B'nai Brith), or by reputable national associations (like National Geographic) who bring decades of experience and expertise to the trip. Other well-established outfits include Senior Tours (800-227-1100 or www.seniortours.com), and Road Scholar (formerly Elderhostel, reachable at 800-454-5768 or www.roadscholar.org); both cater to solo travelers as well as couples and larger groups.

CHAPTER 5

An Apple a Day

Two of the obstacles most likely to prevent you from having a happy, fulfilling retirement are health problems (which can interfere with your ability to carry out ADLs to the point that you require assisted living or nursing home care) and money problems (which can prevent you from paying for amenities—including in-home care—that you need to live safely on your own). In chapter 1, we discussed strategies for managing finances to enable you to age in place through your 80s and beyond. In this chapter, we discuss health issues.

If access, opportunities, and services are the three pillars of successful aging in place, good medical care might well be the most important service of all. And the key to maintaining good health is being proactive. We know it's difficult—we struggle with this as well—but you should try to make lifestyle changes (like healthier eating habits) that prevent illnesses from occurring in the first place. If symptoms appear, deal with them quickly: not all diseases are treatable, but most can be managed more effectively if you catch them sooner rather than later.

Your Health Care Support Team

Nothing screams "old age" louder than an endless list of medical appointments. It's tempting to want to avoid having regular physical exams (after all, if you don't see the doctor, you can't be told you have a problem), but in this situation ignorance is not bliss. Most medical conditions are easier to treat if they're diagnosed early, and some types of illnesses (like certain cancers) are untreatable if you wait too long.

>> PHYSICIAN ASSISTANTS

Physician assistants (PAs) are health care professionals who perform many (not all) of the tasks performed by MDs: they take medical histories, order and interpret medical tests, perform examinations, make referrals to specialists, and prescribe medications. The profession came into existence in the 1960s in response to the limited availability of MDs in certain regions of the country (primarily rural and impoverished areas); now PAs are common even in wealthier urban settings. Many people—especially those of us who grew up in a world where the "family doc" was the final authority on all things medical—are reluctant to see a PA for checkups and other medical needs, but don't be. PAs undergo rigorous training in most of the same areas as physicians, and in many medical schools first-year medical students and first-year PA students actually take the same classes together. In 2010, patients in the United States made more than 250 million visits to PAs; more than 350 million medication prescriptions were written by PAs that year.

PAs can be a great component of a health care team for people of any age, but they're particularly helpful if you want to age in place in an area (for example, a rural locale) where physicians are few, and those who are established may be in such high demand that they cannot take on new patients because they're overcommitted. You can learn more about PA training and certification through the American Academy of Physician Assistants (AAPA), the national association that oversees PA training, certification, and practice. They can be reached at 703-836-2272, or online at www.aapa.org.

Medical care becomes less frightening if you think of your physician as your partner in health rather than the bearer of potential bad news. But your physician can't do it alone, and you may need to partner with other health professionals as well (a physical therapist, perhaps, or a visiting nurse). Here are the some key players on your health care support team.

PHYSICIAN

As medicine advances and the array of available treatments continues to grow, new medical specialties have flourished. In addition to your primary care physician, your medical team may include oncologists (who specialize in treating cancer), endocrinologists (diabetes and other metabolic disorders), nuclear medicine specialists (targeted radiation and related treatments), physiatrists (movement and pain management), orthopedists (joint and movement disorders), gastroenterologists (digestive disorders), pulmonologists (lung problems), cardiac and vascular specialists (disorders of the heart and blood vessels), urologists (urinary issues), podiatrists (disorders of the foot), and ophthalmologists (eye diseases). Nowadays things have gotten so specialized that there are actually specialties within specialties— surgeons who focus on a specific organ system, for example, and oncologists who specialize in treating a particular type of cancer.

PHARMACIST

Thanks to intensive research and development efforts during the past several decades, medications have become far more effective, with fewer side effects. Medication treatments have also gotten more complicated and more expensive. A pharmacist's job might look simple, but there's much going on behind the scenes. Your pharmacist not only fills prescriptions, but also checks for interactions among different medications (including over-the-counter drugs), and looks for "red flags" from your health history that could signal possible adverse reactions or unanticipated side effects. (You can also check for harmful drug interactions using the Institute for Safe Medication website, www.consumermedsafety.org, which allows you to enter your prescriptions and other information and then flags adverse drug combinations.)

Online and mail-order prescription services are particularly helpful if your mobility is impaired, or you don't have access to a nearby pharmacy. In these situations, mail-in and online prescription refill services can be an important component of your overall plan for aging in place.

Mail-in and online prescription services always have phone, email, and "live chat" options so you can ask questions about your prescriptions,

>> WHEN *NOT* TO READ THE FINE PRINT

Unless you've been trained in pharmacology, drug testing, statistical modeling, and experimental design, you'll likely find it hard to grapple with the pages of data (the legendary "fine print") that now accompany virtually every medication. That listing of possible side effects must, by law, include every symptom ever noted by any participant in a medication's clinical trials—whether or not these symptoms were actually due to the medication. Given this requirement, it's not surprising that everything from aspirin to chemotherapy seems to cause nausea, vomiting, dizziness, dry mouth, blurred vision, constipation, impotence, and fainting. They do—if your clinical trials include thousands of people followed over many months and you have to report every symptom they experience during the trial, drug-related or not.

Though virtually every side effect that could be reported has been, it's also true that some side effects are more frequent (and more serious) than others. That's how to read the fine print: don't just note adverse reactions—note those that occur most commonly, and especially those with significant health implications. (Dry mouth doesn't qualify, increased incidence of stroke does.)

What if you're one of those people who find that reading the endless list of possible adverse effects makes you so anxious you cannot bring yourself to take a needed drug? Don't just toss the prescription if your doctor thinks you would benefit from it. Instead, ask your pharmacist or physician about the most common side effects, and what you should do if any occur. Then hold on to that package insert with the long list of adverse reactions—but stop obsessing over it.

just as you would your local pharmacist. In fact, many people actually find it easier to ask questions online than face-to-face, since not all medication side effects are pretty (and some can be a bit embarrassing).

PHYSICAL THERAPIST

Because joint and movement problems tend to increase with age, and mobility (as we discussed in chapter 4) is crucial to successful aging in place, access to a good physical therapist is an important consideration. Physical therapy can reduce pain, increase mobility, improve balance, and help prevent falls and other injuries. More than most other treatments, physical therapy requires an active partnership between therapist and patient, as the patient is actually doing most of the "work"—some of it right there in the office, using exercise, stretching, massage, mild electrical stimulation, and heat and cold treatments—but much of it at home, through movement and flexibility exercises performed between treatment sessions.

DIETITIAN/NUTRITIONIST

Dietitians provide advice and education to people with special dietary needs (for example, those with diabetic conditions). To use the title "dietitian" (or "registered dietitian"), the person must have completed appropriate training and been certified by the Academy of Nutrition and Dietetics. Although many dietitians help plan and manage food service in hospitals, nursing homes, and schools, there are also community dietitians (who promote wellness within a particular area), consultant dietitians (who usually practice fee-for-service on an ad hoc basis), pediatric dietitians (who specialize in dietary issues involving children), and gerontological dietitians (who have specialized training in the dietary needs of older adults). Dietitians (especially gerontological dietitians) can be especially helpful if you're at risk for illnesses (like diabetes and hypertension) that are influenced by diet.

Like dietitians, nutritionists provide advice regarding proper diet and nutrition, although the label "nutritionist" is not as well regulated as that of dietitian. (In most states, anyone can use the label "nutritionist," and if you see that title in an advertisement, be aware that it may not indicate any special training or expertise.) If you choose to consult a nutritionist to help manage dietary needs, you should ask about training, certification, and experience before signing on.

VISITING NURSE

Some health-related tasks are difficult to do by yourself—they require the services of a skilled, experienced nurse. Visiting nurses help care for surgical wounds in the days and weeks after surgery, administer injections and infusion treatments, and help manage medical equipment (like ostomies) that, if improperly used, can lead to complications. In decades past, such services were usually done in hospitals or skilled nursing facilities, but increasingly they are managed in the home by nurses who specialize in providing this type of care. Not only are visiting nurses helpful in managing the tasks associated with recovery from injury or illness, they may also be able to spot potential problems (like incipient infections) before these problems become serious. It's a win-win situation: you get to recover in the comfort of your home rather than a hospital bed, and treatment costs are far lower than they would be if the same tasks were performed in a health care facility.

HOME HEALTH AIDE

At times (for example, while recovering from a broken hip), you may need help with your basic ADLs, like bathing, dressing, or using the bathroom. Or you might need help with complex ADLs like shopping, cooking, or running errands. A home health aide's job description is straightforward, but also requires considerable flexibility: the home health aide does whatever is needed to promote good health in the patient. In addition to helping with basic and complex ADLs, home health aides are trained to help those with limited perception or limited mobility get around safely. Some people may need a home health aide on a time-limited basis, when recovering from illness or injury, but others need in-home care on a more permanent basis (if, for example, you experience long-term vision or mobility problems that would otherwise make independent living impossible).

Building Your "Dream Team"

In recent years, we Americans have morphed from passive patients who do what we're told to well-informed "consumers of care." As a result, we now focus on factors such as cost and ease of access in choosing providers. In this respect, we've begun to treat medical care like any other type of service, but there's an important difference as well: most people would agree that—staff friendliness, office décor, and evening office hours notwithstanding—health care is one area in which outcome trumps everything.

MAKING GOOD CHOICES

Hospitals and insurance companies compile records of health care providers' effectiveness in various aspects of patient care, and you can use this information to select treatment professionals who achieve the best outcomes. (These records are public—just check the hospital and insurance company websites.) Based on these data, you should be able to find out how often your surgeon has performed a given procedure, and the percentage of his or her patients who had positive outcomes. You can see if your doctor has ever been censured by a hospital board or removed from an insurance panel. You can even read other patients' comments about their treatment experiences and their ratings of their physician.

As you might expect, physicians hate these websites, and view them as places where disgruntled patients make false accusations to get back at doctors they simply don't like. (And rightly so—studies confirm that dissatisfied patients are far more likely than satisfied ones to post comments on these websites.)

In selecting a provider, you may run into a dilemma: oftentimes doctors with the best records aren't the nicest people. If forced to choose, you'll probably do well to forego social skills in favor of medical skills. After all, if your surgeon doesn't have the greatest bedside manner but her success rates are high, she's probably a better option than a warmer, nicer doctor with less positive outcomes. In any case, the bottom line: "Best" doesn't necessarily mean "patient friendly," so if you gain access to the finest surgeon in town and feel you're being treated like just another case—just another number—your best response might be to grin and bear it. (Things are a bit different with primary care physicians, however, where empathy and listening skills really do contribute to good physician-patient "fit.")

MANAGING YOUR TEAM

The more you know about your illnesses, procedures you need, medicines you take, and other health issues, the more effectively you can partner with the members of your health care team. Plus, you'll feel a greater sense of control when you understand what's going on, which is important in managing the stress associated with illness (more on that in chapter 8). You'll be better equipped to make choices about what kinds of care you'll need to age in place, and you'll be able to make better plans for "coping in place" when health problems occur if you have a realistic idea of exactly what you're facing.

The good news is, the Internet has made it possible to educate yourself about the basics of virtually any topic quickly and easily. (In the medical arena, we've found www.webmd.com and www.mayoclinic.com to be particularly informative and user-friendly.) Most of the time providers will applaud your efforts to become a more educated, informed health care consumer—competent practitioners are not offended by intelligent, probing questions.

The bad news is, not all the information available online (or in printed material, for that matter) is accurate and reliable. Many "breakthrough findings" reported in popular magazines are still in the developmental stage—earthshaking for a research scientist and great story material for a reporter, but not yet ready for actual clinical use. The newest drug on the market might well prove safe and effective, but keep in mind that those ads you see on TV are just that—ads—and they're intended to sell the product, not to provide a balanced picture of the drug's advantages and risks.

Although competent practitioners are not offended by good questions, they do take offense when you challenge their knowledge and experience based on factoids gleaned from magazines or Internet blogs. They may also be turned off by unrealistic demands for good results. Medical treatment involves risk—nobody really knows what the outcome will be ahead of time. It is the responsibility of the provider to assess the risks and benefits of prospective treatments, to recommend a course of action, and to carry out the agreed-upon intervention appropriately and competently. But no honest physician can ever "guarantee" a specific outcome.

So what can you do to maintain a positive, trusting partnership with your health care providers? Here are several things:

- **Be willing to look at both sides.** Emotions sometimes lead us to focus exclusively on the "pros" or "cons" of a treatment option early in the decision-making process; we think we're willing to consider all sides of the issue, but deep down we're really not. Try to keep an open mind throughout the information-gathering phase, and don't let a friend's negative experience with a certain procedure cause you to rule out that procedure without hearing all the facts.

- **Stay calm.** Providers are human, and they do have feelings even when they're wearing a stethoscope or surgical scrubs. You want honest answers, even if they're not the answers you'd hoped for, and if you overreact (yell, cry, and so on), your health care provider—quite understandably—may shift from honest responding to reassurance and minimization. That's not what you need: where medical issues are concerned, an unpleasant but necessary truth beats false reassurance every time.

- **Own your decisions.** It is natural to want to blame somebody when things don't turn out as hoped. (This is why even the best physicians get sued and malpractice costs are so high.) In today's litigation-happy environment, there are many safeguards in place to ensure that you know what you're getting into before you proceed. Ask questions until you're satisfied, and if new ones arise later, ask those as well. But in the end, it's your life, your health, and it's ultimately your decision.

> You'll be better equipped to make choices about what kinds of care you'll need to age in place, and you'll be able to make better plans for "coping in place" when health problems occur if you have a realistic idea of exactly what you're facing.

Making decisions about medical matters can be stressful, and there's no way to ensure that the process will be completely smooth or easy. Your best bet is to collect and review the available information (including expert advice), and weigh the probable outcomes openly and honestly. Even though you cannot guarantee that everything will go exactly as planned, you'll know that you made a reasoned decision based on solid information.

Coordinating Your Care

If your health is relatively good, it's easy to coordinate your team. But the more complex your health problems, the larger the number of treatment professionals involved. The providers' capacity to work together smoothly is critical (and yes—sometimes health care providers just don't like each other). While your attending physician generally functions as the primary coordinator of care—the "hub" of the medical team—this isn't always the case when multiple specialists are involved.

If your health issues are complex, you might want to consider bringing in extra help to coordinate various aspects of your care. Fortunately, there are two types of allied health professionals who specialize in doing just that: geriatric care managers and patient advocates.

GERIATRIC CARE MANAGERS

Geriatric care managers (sometimes called *case managers*) are usually nurses or social workers with training and experience in coordinating health care for older adults. They help arrange in-home care and other services, coordinate different aspects of care, monitor progress, and oversee transfers among different treatment settings when needed. Because they are well connected within the area, geriatric care managers can cut through a lot of red tape in a relatively short time. Their calls get answered; their messages returned.

Geriatric care managers usually charge a flat fee of $200 or more for the initial assessment, and an average hourly fee of about $75 for additional work. These fees are rarely covered by Medicare or private insurance, and it's a good idea to put fee arrangements in writing before you begin. Sometimes a local Agency on Aging will offer free or subsidized access to a geriatric care manager on a short-term, time-limited basis.

> Geriatric care managers (sometimes called *case managers*) are usually nurses or social workers with training and experience in coordinating health care for older adults. They help arrange in-home care and other services, coordinate different aspects of care, monitor progress, and oversee transfers among different treatment settings when needed.

You can locate geriatric care managers through senior centers and nursing homes in your area. The National Association of Professional Geriatric Care Managers (www.caremanager.org or 520-881-8008) and the National Association of Social Workers (www.naswdc.org or 202-408-8600) also offer referrals and recommendations.

PATIENT ADVOCATES

Patient advocates help patients with serious illnesses address issues related to insurance coverage and eligibility, coordination of insurance benefits, job retention (including leaves of absence), medical debt crises, negotiations with insurers and creditors, and other practical matters. Because they're experienced in navigating the financial and legal bureaucracies of today's health care system, patient advocates can manage these tasks and free patients to focus on the most important thing: their health. People who have worked with patient advocates report that they can provide great comfort, reassurance, and stress relief.

Most patient advocates work on an individual basis, one-on-one with patients and their families, but others lobby at the state and national levels to improve access to health care. Like care managers, patient advocates

>> INTERNET MEDICINE

It sounds new, but the concept of Internet medicine actually dates to the 1960s, when it was called "telemedicine," and involved diagnosis and consultation over the telephone. The technology has changed, but the basic principle hasn't: when patient and physician cannot be present in the same room (as when a needed specialist happens to live in a different part of the country), they consult over the Internet. It's also used by attending physicians to monitor patients in intensive care and consult with colleagues across town when concerns arise. Internet medical services may make choosing to live in a remote area more viable, since you're never more than a click or call away from expert consultation.

Increasingly powerful online communication technology has made Internet medicine far easier (and less expensive) than it once was, and though critics have voiced concerns regarding patient privacy and physician liability, many people believe that Internet medicine will play an increasing role in health care during the coming years. Medical tasks and procedures now performed over the Internet include:

- Accessing and downloading patient information (including online medical records)
- Monitoring vital signs (heart rate, blood pressure, and other patient data can now be transmitted reliably over the Internet)
- Teleradiology (transmission and remote reading of X-rays)
- Tele-endoscopy (visual inspection of a patient's internal organs in real time by a physician in another part of the country)
- Internet diagnosis and consultation (patient and physician meet "face to face" over the Internet, and the physician can consult with distant colleagues in this way as well)

may assist in medical care decision making, helping ensure that patients' rights are respected and their needs are met. You can find patient advocates in your area through the Patient Advocate Foundation (800-532-5274 or www.patientadvocate.org), or through your local Visiting Nurse Association. Patient advocates tend to have access to a broader range of health care providers than do geriatric care managers because they serve a more diverse patient population, but geriatric care managers have the advantage of being well-known by service providers (including hospital administrators and insurance companies) that are particularly relevant to older adults.

Paying for It

It's no secret that health care in America is expensive. The good news is, there are private and government-funded insurance options that help defray many of these costs. Assuming that the 2010 Health Care Reform Act (the "Affordable Care Act") survives various legislative and legal challenges and takes effect in 2014, it will make health care coverage easier to obtain, and harder to lose. The Health Care Reform Act eliminates many of the obstacles (like denial of coverage for preexisting conditions) that have historically prevented otherwise-healthy people from obtaining the insurance protection they need. (You can read up on the details at www.healthcare.gov.)

You should certainly plan on covering some out-of-pocket costs for late-life health care. Almost everyone does, and the US General Accounting Office estimates that the typical 65-year-old today will pay more than $200,000 in out-of-pocket medical costs during retirement. (That estimate rises to almost $380,000 for a person planning to retire at age 65 in 2030.) These are intimidating numbers, but four public and private sources of health care coverage can help make these out-of-pocket costs more manageable: Medicare, Medigap (Medicare supplement insurance), secondary insurance, and veterans' benefits.

>> THE EYES HAVE IT

More than three million older adults in America have significant vision loss; for these people, independent living can be challenging. As with many health-related issues, being proactive is crucial in maintaining good vision. A periodic visit to the ophthalmologist is well worth your time; your ophthalmologist can not only spot early signs of vision impairment and take steps to correct the problem, but eye exams are among the best ways of detecting certain diseases (like diabetes) that have wide-ranging negative effects.

There are four leading causes of vision impairment among older adults today:

- *Macular degeneration* is a condition wherein leaking blood vessels in the back of the eye interfere with central vision (peripheral vision is less strongly affected). Laser therapy to destroy leaking blood vessels is currently the treatment of choice, but studies suggest that a combination of zinc, beta-carotene, and vitamins C and E may be effective in slowing progression of the disease.

- *Cataract* is a clouding of the lens in the front of the eye; risk factors include diabetes, smoking, and prolonged exposure to direct sunlight. More than half of us develop cataracts by age 80, and though the condition is now surgically treatable, costs may be prohibitive for those without excellent insurance.

- *Diabetic retinopathy* is a condition in which blood vessels in the eye break down, leak, or become blocked, gradually leading to vision loss. Laser surgery or a *vitrectomy* procedure (removal of vitreous humor—the jelly-like substance that fills the eyeball) are currently the treatments of choice for diabetic retinopathy; research into pharmaceutical treatment options is ongoing.

- *Glaucoma* results from damage to the optic nerve connecting eye and brain, and symptoms are rarely detected until nerve damage has become substantial. Timely diagnosis is key because the earlier glaucoma is diagnosed, the greater the amount of vision that can be preserved.

MEDICARE

Medicare is a form of insurance designed to defray medical costs for older adults; it also funds medical care for people who are disabled. Medicare comes in four parts. Part A (which is funded by the payroll tax, or "employment tax," paid during a person's working years) covers certain hospital costs and is available to anyone over age 65. Part B, which is available for an additional fee, whether or not the person has Part A coverage, covers aspects of outpatient care. (In 2012, Medicare Part B premiums were $99 per month for most recipients, with a $140 per year Part B deductible.) Part C (also known as *Medicare Advantage Plan*) is available through Medicare-approved private insurance companies, and combines Medicare Parts A and B (it sometimes includes prescription drug coverage as well, depending upon the plan one chooses).

> The US General Accounting Office estimates that the typical 65-year-old today will pay more than $200,000 in out-of-pocket medical costs during retirement. (That estimate rises to almost $380,000 for a person planning to retire at age 65 in 2030.)

Part D (which includes a variety of plans and varying levels of coverage and copayment) covers prescription drug costs.

Medicare Parts C and D involve a range of options, and choices in both areas can be tricky. It may be worthwhile to check with a Certified Financial Planner before deciding whether or not to purchase Medicare Part C, and with your physician before deciding upon a Medicare Part D plan. Keep in mind that Medicare is undergoing many changes as a result of the 2010 Health Care Reform Act, and some of these changes are being phased in over time. Information regarding current benefits and future plans can be found on the federal government's Medicare website (www.medicare.gov), or by calling 800-633-4227.

>> EMERGENCIES: WHO YA GONNA CALL?

Even the best-laid plans rarely work perfectly, and emergency health situations do arise. You can't prevent these from occurring, but you can—and should—have a plan in place ahead of time. Three good options are personal emergency response systems, home monitoring, and the buddy system.

Personal Emergency Response Systems

Personal emergency response systems have been shown to prolong independent living significantly, especially for those forty million Americans with chronic disabilities. While particularly important for people who live alone, these response systems are also useful for those who live with others. (You never know when you'll be by yourself in the house or the yard and need help.)

Since the 1990s, there has been tremendous growth in emergency response system technology, and we've come a long way since actress Edith Fore appeared in that well-known (and oft-lambasted) infomercial some years back. Numerous emergency response options are now available, but the basics are pretty straightforward: You wear a "panic button" device on a neck chain or wristband, so it's accessible at all times. Press the button and a monitoring site will call you by phone (or intercom if you're in assisted living or senior housing) to find out what you need. If you don't answer, help is dispatched automatically. Systems range from simple call-and-dispatch options through sophisticated video and audio monitoring setups. Some home security systems also offer a variety of call options, allowing you to summon firefighters, police, or EMTs at the touch of a button. (Whatever you do, don't tell the dispatcher "I've fallen and I can't get up!" Thanks to Ms. Fore's memorable performance, it's become the senior equivalent of Prince Albert in a can.)

Home Monitoring

With the development of inexpensive and reliable home-monitoring equipment, it is now possible to keep an eye on every part of your house and property 24/7. Fire, smoke, carbon monoxide, and other hazards can be monitored continuously. If you choose, you need never be out of touch with concerned loved ones. You can also activate locks, lights, alarms, and other devices remotely using a handheld device, or through your smartphone. As with any electronic equipment, expert installation and periodic inspection and repair are essential. Plus, you need to learn how to use the system properly: the best home monitoring setup in the world is worthless if you don't know how to activate and deactivate it.

The Buddy System

Sometimes the best safeguards are the simplest. If your health is reasonably good, arranging mutual daily check-ins with a friend or neighbor may be all that you need to feel safe. A quick phone call, email, or text message can help you feel connected, and there's an added benefit as well: recent studies indicate that merely hearing a supportive voice can lower stress hormone levels substantially. Less stress leads to better health and fewer emergencies. (We'll say more about that in chapter 7.)

In some communities, the Agency on Aging will offer free telephone "check-in" services, or connect you with nearby charitable organizations that do. Your local Agency on Aging can provide more information, or you can contact the National Association of Area Agencies on Aging at 202-872-0888, or at www.n4a.org.

MEDIGAP

Medicare supplement insurance (commonly called *Medigap* insurance) is privately funded health care coverage intended to defray some of the costs not covered by Medicare. Medigap policies are "guaranteed renewable"—your insurer cannot refuse to renew your policy as long as you pay your premiums on time and were truthful when you first applied for coverage.

There are ten standard Medigap policies (Plans "A" through "J"), which range from basic coverage through fairly comprehensive service. (The more elaborate plans also cover some of the costs of prescription drugs, emergency care while abroad, preventive care, and in-home care.) Basic benefits that are covered by all ten plans include:

- Medicare Part A coinsurance costs, plus coverage for 365 days after Medicare benefits end
- Part B coinsurance costs
- Three pints of blood per year

Medicare SELECT plans are essentially Medigap policies sold by HMOs, which designate the specific doctors and hospitals you must use in order to get full coverage. Medicare still pays its share of approved charges, but like any HMO, the SELECT plan may not cover services rendered by out-of-network providers.

SECONDARY INSURANCE

Some employers and professional organizations allow you to maintain existing group health coverage post-retirement, until Medicare kicks in (especially helpful if you retire early). Many people also purchase health insurance privately, though costs can be prohibitive, and some policies exclude preexisting conditions. Precisely what is covered by secondary insurance can vary quite a bit, but generally speaking policies are getting increasingly selective every year: more and more services are being excluded or made difficult to access, and larger percentages of the costs are being shifted to the consumer through higher copays and deductibles.

The rules that govern secondary policies differ from those for Medicare and Medigap. Determining who covers what when you have all three policies can be tricky (and spousal benefits are particularly difficult to decipher). Read your policies carefully, and consider getting advice from an insurance counselor familiar with the rules for your state. The consultation won't be free, but it can go a long way toward helping you understand exactly what is covered by each policy.

VETERANS' BENEFITS

Any United States military veteran is eligible for medical care at a Veterans Affairs (VA) medical facility, whether or not their current problems are service related. However, because there are many more veterans than hospital beds at this time (a situation not likely to change during the coming years), priority is given to urgent, acute conditions. Service-related injuries and illnesses are taken next, and veterans with nonurgent problems who can afford to pay for care elsewhere are the lowest priority.

If you are a veteran, be sure to ask about the VA's Special Pension Aid and Attendance program, a relatively new benefit designed to help defray the costs of in-home, assisted living, and nursing home care for veterans and their spouses (even if care needs are not service related). Aid and Attendance benefits in 2012 topped out at $1,704 per month for a veteran, $1,094 per month for a surviving spouse, and $2,020 per month for a couple where both partners required services. To qualify, you must have limited income and modest assets, and ninety days of continuous military service, at least one day of which took place during a VA-defined "period of war" (it's not necessary that you saw combat). These periods are:

- World War II: 12/7/1941 – 12/31/1946
- Korea: 6/25/1950 – 1/31/1955
- Vietnam: 8/5/1964 – 5/7/1975
- Persian Gulf: 8/2/1990 – present

You can obtain information regarding veterans' benefits from the Veterans Affairs website (www.va.gov) or by calling 800-827-1000. Contact information for local veterans' services (including local VA contact information) is usually listed in the Human Services section of the phone book (look under "Veterans").

There's no doubt about it: good health care is essential for maximizing your quality of life. While most of us must eventually cope with health problems of one kind or another—especially as we move through later adulthood—these challenges need not prevent successful aging in place. Where late-life health is concerned, a bit of planning, flexibility, and honest self-reflection go a long way.

>> FAMILY HEALTH CARE DECISIONS ACTS

Denial can be a powerful thing: though most people know they should put their preferences in writing through health care proxy documents and living wills, fewer than half of American adults actually have one in place. Needless to say, this creates a difficult situation when someone becomes incapacitated unexpectedly (think Terry Schaivo, or—if you remember back a ways—Karen Ann Quinlan). Medical emergencies without proxy documents in place are not only emotionally overwhelming, but they can be financially devastating as well.

Family Health Care Decisions Acts (FHCDAs), which vary from state to state (not all states have them), establish clear rules by which surrogate decision makers can be appointed quickly in an emergency. While the acts do not address every possible situation, they do increase the likelihood that the incapacitated person's beliefs and best interests will be foremost in everyone's mind when health care or end-of-life decisions must be made. In addition to kinship and marriage, FHCDAs also recognize the importance of nontraditional partnerships, friendship bonds, and other longstanding relationships. (Having said this, we still advise you to put in place a health care proxy, living will, and durable power of attorney for health care as soon as possible, if they're not in place already; for details, see chapter 1.)

PART 2

Making It Count

CHAPTER 6

Healthy Mind

In chapters 1 through 5, we discussed practical issues that help set the stage for a secure retirement—money matters, housing, accessibility, and health. Now we can look toward the good stuff. You've worked hard, planned well, and because of this, you have the freedom to decide what you want to do during your retirement—how you'd like to spend your time. The possibilities are endless (and as the years go by your interests might change as well—nothing's written in stone). Just to get started, how about:

- **Taking a course.** Now's the time to explore a new area, perhaps something you didn't have a chance to learn about when you were younger. One of us has always regretted not taking a course in astronomy when he was in college (he was too busy bombing out of the premed program); taking that class is at the top of his list of retirement must-dos. Many colleges and universities offer adult education classes for retirees and other nontraditional students.

- **Writing a book.** It's a daunting task, and quite a time commitment (trust us on that), but there's never been a better time to hit the keyboard. Selling your work to a mainstream publisher can be a challenge unless you have special expertise in some area, but improvements in technology have made self-publishing easier than ever. You might not sell a million (or even a thousand copies), but then again, you never know. A number of best sellers started out as self-published books, including *What Color Is Your Parachute?* and John Grisham's *A Time to Kill* (which he initially hawked from the trunk of his car).

- **Mastering a new skill.** For some, it might be a cooking class; for others it's backgammon or bridge. In many ways, this is the ideal phase of life to venture into uncharted territory: it may take a bit of extra effort to acquire certain skills as you move through your 60s and beyond (we'll discuss these challenges later in this chapter), but you don't have the crowded schedule you had when you were 20 or 30. If learning conversational Spanish takes longer now than it would have a few decades ago, who cares? You've got the time.

- **Riding the web.** Maybe you've thought about starting your own website; if not, you can blog—it's easy (and free). The amazing thing about putting yourself out there on the World Wide Web is it really is "worldwide" (so it doesn't take much oomph to make an impact in the online universe). Even if your interests only resonate with a tiny portion of the online population (seventeenth-century Afghan pottery, anyone?), that's still a lot of people.

- **Reviving an old interest.** One of us used to knit (though she hasn't done it in years). One of us was an art major in college; for a time he painted in oils and acrylics, just for fun. But as we worked to establish our careers, things got busy; like many people we let our hobbies take a back seat to more pressing, practical matters. Item #1 on our retirement checklist is revisiting these (and other) old interests, now that we'll have the time.

Those are just a few possibilities; as we focus on Making It Count in chapters 6 through 10, others will emerge. In this chapter, we discuss things you can do to maximize and maintain your cognitive skills throughout your retirement years so you can take that class or write that book. Let's get started.

>> SELF-PUBLISHING DOS AND DON'TS

As with any industry that has a potentially large clientele and is more or less completely unregulated, the world of self-publishing has its share of scammers and cheats. How, then, do you distinguish the good from the bad? Keep these six things in mind:

- **Work with a reputable organization.** Two of the most reputable are www.amazon.com, which has a platform that enables authors to self-publish their work on Kindle, and Barnes & Noble (www.barnesandnoble.com), which allows authors to self-publish on Nook. Both provide plenty of step-by-step instruction to guide you through the process.

- **Avoid vanity presses.** There are dozens of companies that are more than happy to take your money and print copies of your book. Why shouldn't they be? It's an easy way to make a buck, and many charge hundreds—even thousands—of dollars to do work that other, more reputable companies will do for far less. Two well-established companies that have a good reputation are lulu.com and CreateSpace, a subsidiary of amazon.com (www.createspace.com). Any outfit that requires you to pay a large up-front fee should be avoided. If a company makes promises regarding sales volume that sound too good to be true, they are.

- **Use social media to get your message out.** Aside from being talented, most successful self-published authors have one thing

Minding Your Mind: When Things Go Right

Stereotypes notwithstanding, late life is not invariably a time of cognitive decline. Some skills do tend to deteriorate with age, but others actually strengthen. We'll begin with the positive:

- **Experience.** Experience is the bedrock of learning in adulthood—it provides the foundation upon which new skills are built. Having "been there, done that" not only enables you to anticipate what's coming next, but also provides context for new information—perspective that in common: they leveraged social media to get the word out on their book. They blogged, tweeted, created a Facebook page—and more. Create an Author Page on amazon.com, and ask people who've read your book to post reviews.

- **Be prepared to do some legwork.** If you're truly committed to reaching as large an audience as possible (and if you're not, you probably shouldn't be doing this), you'll need to pound the pavement a bit. Many booksellers will stock copies of books by local authors; some will sponsor readings or signings as well. Offer to give free copies of your book to members of a book club—and then offer to attend when they discuss your work. Nothing is more valuable than word-of-mouth in selling books.

- **Write about what you know.** It sounds obvious, but it's important. Don't write about what you think people are interested in, write about what you love. You'll have a better chance of penning a successful tome if you take that route—and if it doesn't sell many copies the time was still well spent: you were writing about something that fascinated you anyway.

- **Set the bar high.** Only put your work out there when it's the very best it can be. Oftentimes it takes multiple drafts, and many edits, before a first effort is polished enough for public consumption. Resist the urge to write that final sentence and celebrate—if you want your book to be as good as it can be, the real work is just beginning. . .

a younger person might not have. Live long enough and you'll rarely be taken by surprise. (Let's face it—was "Occupy Wall Street" really all that new? Not to those of us who remember the 1960s.)

- **Perspective.** Perspective allows to you focus on the big picture so you can distinguish what's really important in the long run from what just seems pressing at the moment. Because perspective helps you sort out the impact of events large and small, it enables you to plan more effectively and react less impulsively. Perspective helps us put long-term gain before short-term gratification—and we make better decisions as a result.

- **Wisdom.** The world is full of people who are smart but not wise (think Richard Nixon). Intelligence enables you to learn, acquire new information, and think logically—but that's it. Wisdom is the ability to bring your unique perspective to a situation, blending information and logic with your personal values so your decisions are not merely correct, but also morally sound and good. People of all ages can be intelligent, but wisdom comes with the deeper, more nuanced understanding of the world that only experience and perspective can provide.

Cognitive Changes Normal to Aging

The brain is an amazing thing: no wonder Woody Allen said it was his second-favorite organ. Your brain has the capacity to store an infinite number of facts (literally), and carry out multiple tasks simultaneously (so you can walk, have a snack, look in store windows, and carry on a conversation at the same time). Your brain is always developing new connections (even in your 70s and beyond), is capable of coming up with novel solutions to vexing problems, and every once in a while it does something truly magnificent (think $E = MC^2$, Van Gogh's self-portraits, and Sergeant Pepper).

For the most part, your 80-year-old brain will work pretty much like your 20-year-old brain did. But there are some expectable changes as well. Just as Woody's most favorite organ probably doesn't function at 80 exactly as it did when he was 20 (we're just speculating here), to maximize the power of an aging brain, you'll need to understand how it's evolving. A few key changes are worth noting, so you can anticipate them and adapt:

- **Things take longer.** Though your mind is overflowing with information, it may take longer to find it now. Retrieval speed slows with age, so it takes more time to access facts, both personal (like your brother's birthday) and abstract (what's the capital of Iowa?). It may take longer to formulate a response as well: although our store of knowledge (what researchers call *crystallized intelligence*) increases as we age, our ability to "think on our feet" and react quickly (what researchers call *fluid intelligence*) diminishes. Add to these changes some experience-related factors—studies show that older adults deliberately hold back before blurting out a response, making sure they know exactly what they want to say before they say it—and you'll likely find that you've slowed a bit in your reactions. There are many areas in life in which a quick response isn't necessary, so this slowing isn't altogether bad. But it can be an obstacle in situations where fast judgment and rapid response are essential (like driving).

- **It's harder to focus.** With age, our ability to divide our attention diminishes, and it becomes more difficult to filter out irrelevant information and carry out multiple tasks at once. Kids can walk down the street texting all the way; we advise you not to try that (unless you enjoy tripping and falling). As we age, we tend to shift from free-form multitasking to more linear, step-by-step processing, completing one task and "filing it away" before we move on to the next. Though this may on occasion evoke eye rolls of contempt from impatient waiters, it's actually a reasonable way to maximize brainpower and minimize errors.

- **Practice makes perfect.** If you've ever spent time around young children, you know that kids are capable of absorbing information with amazing efficiency—their sponge-like gray matter literally soaks up everything that's going on around them. The older you get, the harder you have to work to encode new memories and lay down new neural pathways (which is how knowledge is actually "stored"). As a result, you must now take a more active approach to learning. Repetition is crucial; practice is key. Processing new information through multiple modalities (visual, verbal, movement-related) becomes more important. There's some irony in this: even as your mental energy tends to wane a bit with age, you must expend more of it to achieve the same results. (Here's one place where your experience and perspective can come in handy: they'll enable you to endure the increased effort required to acquire new skills—both in you, and in those around you—with patience and grace.)

>> ADULT EDUCATION

Some retirees attend college to obtain a two-year or four-year degree, and if that's one of your goals, bravo! Go for it. But taking classes to obtain a degree is not your only option; many schools offer adult education courses at night (or on the weekend), for nontraditional, part-time students. It might also be possible for you to enroll in or audit a regular undergraduate class if what you're hoping to study isn't available through the adult education program. (Some colleges allow this, others don't.)

Both options have their advantages. Adult education classes usually address material on a less technical, more accessible level (you probably won't need a calculator), and they tend to move at a more measured pace. On the other hand, regular undergraduate classes address a much broader array of topics, and you're more likely to find one that matches your interests.

If you do take an undergraduate class, be advised—things have changed. We're not just talking about the nose rings and other facial piercings here (and be advised that most 20-year-olds today have tattoos). You should also be prepared for the fact that college culture has changed, and the classroom experience has followed suit. A few things to keep in mind:

- **Most courses have websites.** The syllabus will be posted here, as will the required journal articles and book chapters. (The era of checking out reserve readings at the library is gone.) Many professors

Proactive Interventions: Use It or Lose It

Accommodating the brain's changes is important, but there are things you can do to maintain your cognitive health, maximize mental ability, and slow the neural aging process. The sharper your wits, the more you can accomplish—and the more you'll enjoy it as well.

use course websites to post announcements as well, or have online discussions about class material. Most course websites are quite user-friendly, and colleges typically provide online or "helpdesk" support if you get stuck.

- **Textbooks cost $100+.** This stems in part from the fact that textbooks have pictures (and those with color pictures are especially pricey). Fortunately, you can buy many textbooks used at the college or university bookstore, or through online booksellers—just Google "used textbooks." (Sidenote: Textbook publishers are on to this, which is why new editions tend to come out every three to four years. It's not that the field has changed appreciably—they just want to make the last edition obsolete.)

- **PowerPoint has replaced the blackboard.** Most classrooms no longer have blackboards at all; they now have "whiteboards," and markers rather than chalk. But few professors use these very much these days. Expect most or all of the material for your courses to be presented via PowerPoint, a high-tech slideshow that integrates text, images, and online media (like clips from YouTube).

- **Everyone texts during class.** It takes some getting used to, but 24/7 texting is now the norm among the college set. Some professors have very strict rules about this, others are more lax, but be prepared to see many of your classmates texting regularly throughout class. (Yes, it's very annoying. Let it go.)

EXERCISE YOUR MIND

Just as modest exercise helps keep a body strong, even modest mental challenges can help keep your cognitive skills sharp. Crossword and Sudoku puzzles, word searches, video games, and other brain teasers have all been shown to help people maintain their *visual scanning skills* (the ability to identify details in complex images), their verbal and linguistic fluency, and their problem-solving skills. Games that allow you to match your wits against others are particularly helpful (so keep up that weekly mah-jongg or poker game). And couch potatoes take note: turn off the TV every once in a while—daily reading is essential. It doesn't matter what you read (romance novels and science fiction are as good as historical narrative), but it's important to choose things that you enjoy. You're more likely to keep at it that way.

>> ACCESSING FREE CULTURAL EVENTS

Everyone likes a bargain, and if you take advantage of opportunities to attend concerts, lectures, and other events for free, you'll stretch your retirement dollars. Four sources are particularly helpful:

- **Regional websites.** Most cities and towns have them (in rural areas they may be county websites instead). Regional websites are great sources for free (or inexpensive) events like farmers' markets, festivals, and holiday concerts. When we lived in Gettysburg, the Apple Harvest Festival was a highlight of each autumn; in Syracuse, the New York State Fair was huge.

- **Museums and concert venues.** Many advertise free concerts or docent-led museum tours (and sometimes these programs are quite extensive). Some concert halls have a series of free events, but those that don't often allow the public to attend concert rehearsals before opening night. (You'll likely find these advertised on the concert hall website.) Some venues will let you attend performances for free if you volunteer to work as an usher at the event.

- **Colleges and universities.** Beyond regular courses and adult education classes, many colleges and universities have lecture series, concert series, dance recitals, and dozens of other free cultural opportunities. At many larger institutions, there are multiple free events available every night of the week.

- **Bookstores and coffeehouses.** Many bookstores sponsor book readings, poetry readings, and signings, and other "meet the author" events. Locally owned coffeehouses sponsor these types of gatherings, too, as well as free concerts by local musicians who are happy to play for a modest audience to get exposure.

FEED YOUR HEAD

While there are no "magic foods" that fend off aging and preserve your cognitive skills indefinitely, considerable research supports the importance of a healthy, balanced diet rich in proteins and vitamins as a way of promoting health and vitality. Antioxidants can combat the buildup of toxic substances called *free radicals* throughout your body (including your brain). Antioxidants are found in many different foods, but especially good sources include blueberries, cranberries, kidney beans, pinto beans, plums, and red apples. Beyond these dietary changes, it's also important to maintain a healthy weight, avoid (or quit) smoking, moderate your alcohol use, and control your carbohydrate intake. (Yeah, we know: we love pasta too.) WebMD (www.webmd.com) has a good section on eating for longevity, and you can also check out the Healthy Eating for Older Adults section of the Academy of Nutrition and Dietetics website at www.eatright.org (see the Resource and Contact Information section on page 223).

REMAIN ACTIVE

Abundant evidence documents the benefit of exercise in maximizing cognitive capacity. Exercise enhances blood flow to the brain (so neurons get more oxygen), builds muscle mass, improves balance, and increases your baseline energy level, even when you're resting. All these things combine to improve brain, heart, and lung function, reduce the frequency of slips and falls, and enhance overall health. The endorphin rush of exercise can actually brighten your mood and reduce anxiety (more on that in a bit). Staying active also helps combat weight gain, which (aside from preserving your hottie status) will have even more far-reaching consequences for your health than your ego.

STAY CONNECTED

Technology has its limits: even in a world filled with fascinating stuff, people remain our best source for stimulation, challenge, excitement, and the thousand other things that keep us on our mental toes. We'll discuss the health benefits of staying connected in chapter 7 (and strategies for building new relationships post-retirement in chapter 9). For now, keep in mind that the research is clear: those of us who have the most contact with other people on a regular basis tend to be the most verbally fluent, mentally alert, and—most important of all—happiest.

Minding Your Mind: When Things Go Awry

Everyone—young or old, rich or poor—encounters obstacles along the way. Living the good life post-retirement not only requires that you be proactive to maintain your cognitive skills, but also that you know when it's best to reach out to others—to understand when you need some extra help to overcome a problem. Depression and anxiety can strike at any age, but people 50 and over are especially susceptible. By age 60, our risk for Alzheimer's disease and other forms of dementia begins to increase. Fortunately, mental health researchers have made tremendous strides in recent years in identifying the early signs of late-life mental illness and developing treatments specifically tailored to the mental health needs of older adults.

The National Institute of Mental Health (NIMH) estimates that upward of 5 percent of older adults are clinically depressed. (That number jumps to 13 percent if you have a serious illness.) To some extent, the symptoms of depression are the same at age 8 as they are at age 80: sadness, hopelessness, lack of energy, difficulty concentrating, trouble sleeping, appetite changes, and loss of interest in things you usually find pleasurable. But there are two symptoms of depression more common in older than younger people:

- **Somatic complaints.** True, people of all ages experience aches and pains when they're depressed, but older adults are more likely than younger adults to have back pain, neck pain, joint pain, or digestive upset. We tend to express psychological discomfort in age-appropriate ways, and for older folks that means physically.

- **Cognitive impairment.** This is common enough that it has a name: *pseudodementia* (literally "false dementia"). Many older adults experience some confusion and disorientation when depressed, and in the past, many were mistakenly diagnosed as having Alzheimer's disease based on physicians' misreading of these symptoms. We've gotten better at distinguishing depression-based pseudodementia from genuine dementia, and treating each appropriately. (See the sidebar on page 120 for advice on identifying pseudodementia in yourself or a loved one.)

Just as most everyone gets the blues on occasion, most everyone also has the occasional episode of worry, fretting about things that might go wrong. Recent studies suggest that anxiety not only increases with age, but with each successive generation as well (so you're more likely than your parents to experience clinically significant anxiety, just as they were more likely to experience it than their parents). Like depression, anxiety tends to be underreported, especially by men, which delays treatment and worsens the problem. More than 10 percent of older adults have an anxiety disorder; these include everything from phobias and generalized ("free floating") anxiety to debilitating panic attacks.

How can you tell if your worries are just worries, or a sign of a more serious problem? Look for these two things:

- **They're unrealistic.** Most people aren't wild about spiders or snakes (you can count us among that group). But there's a difference between being startled when you see a spider in the kitchen and being so fearful that you literally cannot go to sleep until you've checked every corner of the bedroom (including under the bed) for spider activity. Similarly, it's one thing to be anxious about meeting new people, but when this anxiety is so great that you stop going to social events, it's no longer normal—now it's a social phobia.

- **They interfere with your life.** Some people have mild episodes of free-floating anxiety; others have panic attacks so severe that they're literally stopped in their tracks, frozen in fear. If your anxiety approaches that level, it's time to seek help. Similarly, lots of people are anxious about flying, but if you won't take vacations or attend family functions because you're afraid to get on a plane, it might be worth talking to someone about this. You're cheating yourself out of a world of experiences.

Treating Depression and Anxiety

Two interventions—psychotherapy and pharmacotherapy (drug therapy)—have a long history in treating depression and anxiety. A number of effective self-help programs are also available; for people with milder symptoms, these may be useful as well. Here's what you need to know.

PSYCHOTHERAPY

Hundreds of studies confirm that psychotherapy works. Speaking with a therapist about your problems not only helps you feel better, it can literally alter your brain chemistry, helping rebalance neurotransmitter activity and form new neural connections. These new neural pathways enable you to find new ways of responding to longstanding problems—they make it easier to break decades-old habits, and change the way you think, feel, and behave.

Therapy acts on a psychological level as well: numerous studies show that part of what makes psychotherapy effective is the therapeutic relationship itself. A trained therapist not only helps you focus on the key issues in your life, but also creates an accepting, nonjudgmental environment that facilitates growth and positive change. A therapist can help you enhance coping, communication, and interpersonal skills that impact positively on many interactions. The most well-established therapies (sometimes called *evidence-based therapies*) are usually covered by health insurance (including Medicare and Medicaid), making them accessible to retirees with modest nest eggs.

PHARMACOTHERAPY

Psychopharmacology (the study of drugs and their effects on mood and behavior) has been one of the most productive areas of science during the past several decades, and the latest developments in drug treatment for psychological disorders have been nothing short of remarkable. By boosting the effects of certain brain chemicals and dampening the impact of others, the newest *psychotropic* (mood-altering) medications improve mental functioning, increase energy levels, and help regulate appetite and sleep patterns. The best can do this without some of the adverse effects common in older mood-altering drugs (dry mouth, nausea, digestive problems, loss of sexual drive).

Keep in mind that—TV ads notwithstanding—even the safest psychotropic drugs have certain risks, and some side effects can be quite serious, so your responses to these medications must be monitored closely by your doctor. If you take antidepressants or *anxiolytics* (medications that reduce anxiety), be sure to report any changes in health, mood, or behavior, even those that seem trivial. Never increase or decrease medication dosages unless expressly advised to do so, and if you do have to alter your regimen, follow the prescribed change schedule precisely. Also be sure to follow any dietary restrictions (including prohibitions against alcohol) while on these medications; failure to do so may undermine the medication's impact, or cause significant adverse reactions.

SELF-HELP

For certain types of problems, a self-help program can be useful (either by itself or in combination with more traditional treatments). Alcoholics Anonymous has helped countless people overcome alcohol addiction over the years; Narcotics Anonymous, though newer, is effective as well. Many hospitals, community centers, and senior centers offer support groups to help people deal with specific life changes and transitions (retirement, widowhood), mental or physical illnesses (depression, diabetes), and other challenges (overeating, gambling problems, recovery from abuse).

There are also a number of self-help books available for combating depression, anxiety, and other common problems. These tend to be most helpful for people whose symptoms are fairly mild. (If you experience depression or anxiety that is debilitating, psychotherapy and medication are better choices than self-help.) If you do decide to go the self-help route, be sure to do your homework, and purchase a book based on science rather than myth. The credentials of the author will tell you a lot in this regard, and if the book is published by the American Psychiatric Association, American Psychological Association, or some other reputable organization, that should give you added confidence as well.

Identifying and Managing Dementia

In contrast to depression and anxiety, which stem from a combination of biological and environmental factors, Alzheimer's disease and other forms of dementia are neurological disorders. That doesn't mean that lifestyle is irrelevant—things like diet and smoking can have a significant impact, as longstanding hypertension increases the likelihood of developing vascular dementias. A history of head injuries (as might result from playing field hockey or football) also increases dementia risk. On the other hand, some lifestyle factors actually seem to *preserve* cognitive functions; a long-term study of Catholic nuns who devoted their lives to contemplation, teaching, and service documented the impact of lifestyle in maintaining robust cognitive skills into very advanced age. (Daily reading, writing, and socializing all helped.)

Though dementia itself is neurological, how dementia gets expressed—the form its symptoms take—is influenced by personality. One common consequence of dementia is *disinhibition*—exaggeration of longstanding personality traits and behavioral tendencies (so the assertive person may become downright aggressive as they become more neurologically impaired, and the mildly suspicious person may become truly paranoid).

There are many forms of dementia; combined they affect over four million people in the United States. Over 2.5 million Americans suffer from Alzheimer's disease, with 12 percent of 84-year-olds developing Alzheimer's disease or some other form of dementia. (By age 89, that number increases to 25 percent). Those are intimidating figures, to be sure, but you can look at it the other way around as well: even as we approach age 90, the majority of us are dementia-free.

Still, it's important to be informed about dementia's warning signs and symptoms (we describe these in the sidebar on page 124). Unfortunately, there is no proven preventive measure available at present, nor is there an effective cure. That said, everyone's experience is different, and while some people with dementia decline rapidly, others maintain reasonably good cognitive functioning for years. We're getting better at managing dementia's symptoms as well, so while you cannot prevent Alzheimer's disease from affecting you or a loved one, you may be able to slow the progression of the disease, or mitigate some of the losses, especially during the early phases of the illness.

So what should you do if you or a loved one shows signs of dementia? First, don't panic. There are some rare instances in which a person with Alzheimer's disease declines very rapidly after being diagnosed, but that's the exception rather than the norm. For most people, losses are quite gradual. Three interventions—medication, accommodation, and caregivers—can help moderate the effects of dementia; these interventions, alone or in combination, allow you to maintain your independence and maximize cognitive function as long as possible.

>> COGNITIVE CHANGES THAT INDICATE A PROBLEM

There is considerable variation in how dementia is expressed, but there are some "red flags" that almost always signal trouble. If you see these in yourself or a loved one, take action: make an appointment with your doctor, and if your doctor suspects a problem, consider seeing a psychologist as well, for a thorough cognitive assessment. Four types of difficulties are particularly worrisome:

- **Persistent memory deficits.** If you cannot remember things that people say to you after only a few seconds have passed, this suggests the start of a significant memory problem. Sometimes we don't notice (or don't want to notice) this in ourselves, so the first clue may be in others' reactions. When people voice annoyance because you're saying the same things over and over, or complain that they have to repeat themselves because you're not paying attention, take it seriously—especially if you hear it from several different people.

- **Disorientation.** Almost everybody has had the experience of entering a room and forgetting what they came for, or driving down the highway and briefly "blanking" on where they're headed. These "senior moments" usually clear in a few seconds, but if they don't—

MEDICATION

Medications called *cholinesterase inhibitors* (cholinesterase is a neurotransmitter) have shown some success in improving memory, attention, reasoning, and language use in people with dementia. These medications increase mental energy as well, and improve social interaction. It's important to note that, despite what TV ads may imply, cholinesterase inhibitors can slow the progression of dementia symptoms, but they do not stop or reverse them. We're still early in the research process, so no long-term data on the effectiveness of these medications are available. However, they may be a promising intervention for helping manage the initial symptoms of Alzheimer's disease and other dementias.

if you find that you're confusing night and day, month, season, or time of year, that's a red flag. If you feel lost in familiar settings (like your own neighborhood), or you're unsure of the location of familiar destinations, something's wrong.

- **Speech difficulties.** We all forget names occasionally, or draw a blank when trying to recall a word or phrase. However, if your speech is peppered with "whatchamacallit" and "whatshername," it's a problem. If you cannot retrieve familiar information no matter how hard you try, even when you use those cueing techniques that have jogged your memory successfully in the past, seek help.

- **Problems with executive function.** Forgetting where you put your keys is not a sign of dementia; forgetting how to use them might be. Not remembering all the items in a dish you make regularly could reflect fatigue or distraction; not remembering how to use the oven to cook that dish suggests a more serious problem. The formal term for inability to remember how things are used is a *deficit in executive function*. It's a sign of significant cognitive problems. In fact, more than memory deficits themselves, it's usually problems with executive function that prevent a person from living on their own safely, and cause the person to require a higher level of care.

ACCOMMODATION

Beyond medication, it's often helpful to devise a series of prompts and cues that help the person with dementia access needed information. This is one area in which new technology can be a real lifesaver. You can use smartphones, tablets, and computers to store lists of names, addresses, phone numbers, and email addresses, accompanied by pictures, captions, descriptions, and any other information that might be helpful (pictures work especially well as memory aids). Global Positioning Systems (GPS devices) can get you from place to place with turn-by-turn instructions—helpful in navigating unfamiliar territory (and comforting in familiar territory as well, in case you get confused). Low-tech can be helpful, too: you can always get the date, time, weather, and traffic conditions from your TV or radio. And don't discount the importance of tried-and-true "no-tech" options either—writing down lists of reminders, and using calendars and daily planners to stay on track.

<blockquote>

>> LIVING ALONE AS MEMORY FADES: SOME ADDITIONAL PRECAUTIONS

Medication along with various accommodations (like prompts and cues) are important for anyone whose memory is not what it once was, but they're especially important for people who live on their own, without the added protection of a roommate or partner close at hand. In these situations, a few additional suggestions for safe aging in place are in order:

- Personal emergency response systems will be especially important here, so you can summon help if needed.
- You might want to arrange periodic check-ins through your local Agency on Aging, Senior Center, or other organization.
- Housekeeping service (if you can afford it) can also serve as a periodic safety check (with the added benefit of some extra help keeping the house in order).
- If feasible, it may be wise to opt for apartment living in lieu of a private home (and for a senior community or NORC in lieu of independent living).

</blockquote>

CAREGIVERS

The ultimate memory aid is the presence of another person who's there to help. This may in fact be the most common accommodation for dementia. It's certainly the one with the longest history: when extended families were the norm, younger family members cared for older relatives; it was expected.

A trusted caregiver not only keeps the dementia patient safe, but also provides companionship, comfort, and social interaction. Hiring a formal caregiver tends to be the most expensive option, unfortunately, and unless you have a good long-term care insurance policy, this option may be out of reach (remember from chapter 5 that Medicare doesn't cover the cost of most in-home care). But that's okay: for married or cohabiting older adults, an ideal solution is for the higher-functioning person to act as caregiver for the less well-functioning person. Sometimes each member of a couple has different limitations (one person might have failing memory, the other mobility problems), and in these situations each partner can "fill in the gap" for the other. Children, siblings, friends, and trusted neighbors can help out as well; caregiving works best when it's a team effort. Sometimes a bit of extra help from someone you trust is exactly what you need to age in place.

Some Closing Thoughts

Alzheimer's disease can have devastating effects on the individual and his or her family—there's no doubt about that. But people with dementia can—and should—experience life to its fullest, to the degree that it's safe to do so. Failing memory need not prevent a person from enjoying their fiftieth wedding anniversary, their granddaughter's confirmation, or their nephew's bar mitzvah. Even if they're confused about the details, joining the family for Thanksgiving or attending a neighborhood holiday party can still be pleasurable. Impairments in speech may prevent the dementia patient from telling you how much they enjoy the occasional dinner out, but you shouldn't assume that means they aren't enjoying it.

So think of dementia (or for that matter, depression) as one more of life's challenges—something that requires flexibility and adaptation on your part, but need not prevent you from getting the most out of your retirement years. "Making it count" doesn't mean making it count only when the going's easy, but also when obstacles arise. Like many things in life, sometimes the journey is a little more rewarding if you actually have to work at it.

Think of it this way: if you or a loved one has failing vision or mobility problems, you deal with those challenges and continue to live your life. So it is with dementia: you do the best you can as you play the cards you've been dealt.

CHAPTER 7

Healthy Body

If I'd known I was gonna live this long, I'd have taken better care of myself.
—EUBIE BLAKE, AT AGE 100

Money can't buy health; health is priceless. As we discussed in chapter 1, certain aspects of our health are beyond our control—if diabetes runs in your family, there's nothing you can do about that. But whatever risk factors you may have, they are just that: *risk* factors. Though you can't make these risk factors disappear, you can behave in ways that maximize your well-being and move you toward the healthy end of your "risk factor spectrum."

The better your health, the broader your range of post-retirement opportunities: opportunities to travel, mentor others, become involved in charitable work or local politics—you name it. Devoting some time and effort to maximizing your health and wellness is well worth it. Even if you've never been proactive in this area before, you can still make a difference now: it's never too late to start.

In this chapter, we talk about maintaining good health throughout your retirement, maximizing wellness, and coping with illness when it occurs.

Health and Wellness

Years ago a colleague told us about a patient she had been treating—a man in his 40s who had recently been diagnosed with a terminal illness. She went on to describe her patient's approach to his illness: he was tying up loose ends, of course, but he was also cherishing the time he had left, spending it wisely, and making mindful choices about how best to live each day. He became actively involved in a foundation that raised funds to support research on his illness, pancreatic cancer, not just donating money but contributing his time to help with the day-to-day functioning of the organization. His attitude and outlook were resolutely positive, and rather than leaning on others for support, he was the strong one, offering reassurance (and a shoulder to cry on) to his wife and young son.

Our colleague made a remark that seemed strange at the time; now it makes perfect sense. Her patient, she said, was very sick, yet in many ways he was also very well.

Health and wellness: they're not the same thing. The Merriam-Webster dictionary defines health as "the condition of being sound in body and mind; freedom from physical disease or pain." Capturing the key features of wellness is a bit trickier, but most widely accepted definitions emphasize that—more than merely the absence of illness—wellness is a state of physical, mental, and spiritual well-being, exemplified by quality of life and a sense of personal satisfaction. Wellness is a lifestyle wherein one makes thoughtful, careful choices about healthy living, and is always on the lookout for ways to improve.

> Wellness is a lifestyle wherein one makes thoughtful, careful choices about healthy living, and is always on the lookout for ways to improve.

So there you are, and here's a bit of advice. You can't prevent yourself from getting sick—it happens. But no matter how good (or bad) your health, you can choose to be well.

>> HEALTH CARE COLLECTIVES

A number of health care corporations have experimented with the concept of grouping providers and services in the same facility—kind of like an outpatient mall. You may find an internist, cardiologist, ophthalmologist, psychologist, pharmacy, radiology clinic, physical therapy/rehab center, dietitian, and a host of other specialists all under one roof (or in one strip mall). It's actually a great health care model, as you may be able to "bundle" appointments and trips, cut down on information exchange hassles, and facilitate communication among providers.

Informal health collectives have also been springing up here and there: a group of friends or neighbors will contract with a provider for a discount rate in exchange for the guarantee of "bulk" business. If the group is large enough, and members live near each other, as in a naturally occurring retirement community (NORC), the provider may be willing to come to you rather than the other way around. Due to the intricacies of health insurance law, this system tends to work best for services paid out-of-pocket, but if the provider is willing to work through some legal and procedural details with insurance companies, coverage may be similar to that rendered in a standard office setting. Generally speaking, in locales where there's a lot of competition for clients, you're more likely to find providers willing to make such deals.

If you go this route, you'll want to begin by determining whether there are enough people in your NORC to warrant a "collective home visit"; six to eight is usually the minimal number to make it worth a physician's time (and keep in mind that everyone involved must be available on the same day, and be flexible enough that the physician can schedule consecutive appointments). Once that's in place, it's time to contact physicians who might be interested in participating. They'll need to accept Medicare, of course, and in general a group practice is best because of the additional staffing and scheduling flexibility it affords. Some visiting physicians prefer to be accompanied by a nurse, or someone else familiar with their routine who can help with the details, call in orders, and contact office staff.

The New Forty

Advances in health care have extended our lives in ways our great-grandparents never could have imagined. Life expectancy for women born in 1900 was 51 years, and that for men was 48. Women and men born in 1953—people who are about 60 years old now—can expect to live well into their 70s or beyond. Times have changed indeed.

Sixty may be the new 40, but time takes its toll. There are things we can do to slow the aging process and maintain health and wellness throughout our retirement years, but doing so takes effort (eating well, exercising regularly). This may require some lifestyle changes, as we discuss in the following section, but the good news is, we're also pretty good at adapting psychologically to the opportunities and challenges of later adulthood. We'll discuss those psychological adaptations in a bit as well.

BETTER LATE THAN NEVER

It's never too late to make changes and improve your health. The earlier you start, the greater the potential benefit, but even small improvements can make big differences—no matter what your age. And though it may seem counterintuitive, for certain types of health-promoting activities, starting later may actually yield gains that are as good as—sometimes better than—the gains that would result if you had started sooner. For example, studies have shown that people who take up wheelchair aerobics in their 70s or 80s actually show greater percentages of muscle mass increase than those who begin at age 60. Go figure. . .

> Though it may seem counterintuitive, for certain types of health-promoting activities, starting later may actually yield gains that are as good as—sometimes better than—the gains that would result if you had started sooner.

Making healthy choices later in life can also yield benefits for serious illnesses that have already onset. Quitting smoking at 50 is great—by doing so you might be able avoid certain disease processes altogether. But even if you're 80 and already being treated for COPD (chronic obstructive pulmonary disease), quitting smoking might enable you to decrease

>> HOUSING AND HEALTH

It's a two-way relationship. One benefit of good health is a broader array of living options, but where we live also affects our health in a variety of ways. Three stand out:

Conditions within the Home

- Hazards like lead paint and mold can impair neurological function (especially in children), and compromise lung function in people of all ages (but especially those who have coexisting conditions like asthma and COPD). If you're unsure, have a home inspector ascertain whether there are any paint or mold problems that require intervention.

- Poorly constructed plumbing increases the possibility of leaks and mold. Poorly constructed gas fixtures are prone to leaks as well, so have these inspected annually. Regardless of what type of heating and cooking systems you have, be sure to install a carbon monoxide detector on every floor of your home.

- Steep staircases lead to trips and falls; substandard heating and cooling systems are associated with increased risk for cardiovascular disease, and can lead to hypothermia or heatstroke when weather conditions become extreme. You can't do much about preexisting stairwells, but inadequate heating and cooling systems should be repaired or upgraded.

Neighborhood Conditions

- Poorer neighborhoods have increased rates of crime and violence; older adults are frequent targets. If you live in a neighborhood where crime is an issue, take precautions when venturing out, especially at night (for example, travel with a friend or in a group).

- The less wealthy the neighborhood, the fewer grocery stores in close proximity (and studies show that grocery stores in poorer neighborhoods tend to have less fresh produce and lower-quality meats than those in wealthier neighborhoods). Consider pooling your resources so several people can make periodic shopping trips to stores with better selections and higher-quality products.
- When neighborhood conditions are poor, crowding increases, and cooperation and trust among area residents tends to decline. Neighborhood watch groups and block associations can help people feel more connected and better protected.

Housing Affordability

- When housing costs are high relative to income, less money is available for health care and other essentials; in extreme circumstances, people must choose between housing costs and other necessities (utilities, food, medication). If less expensive housing is available, it might make sense to move sooner rather than later.

- Less expensive housing often entails a longer commute to work (increased cost, increased stress, less leisure and family time), so if you're working post-retirement, investigate the feasibility of working from home ("telecommuting") one or two days each week.

- Unaffordable housing leads to frequent relocation; residents are at the mercy of landlords who may increase rent with little warning as demand for housing increases. Be sure to know your rights as a resident so you're not squeezed out illegally. These vary from state to state, so check with your local Agency on Aging. (Nolo.com also provides a good overview of issues in this area—you can access this portion of their website at www.nolo.com/legal-encyclopedia /renters-rights).

the amount of medication you take and lower the amount of supplemental oxygen you require as well; both will enhance your quality of life.

Where health is concerned, sooner is better—but later is good, too.

PSYCHOLOGICAL ADAPTATIONS

Aging can't be helped (and the alternative sucks), but fortunately nature has equipped us to cope with the physical challenges of later adulthood. Three processes play an especially important role:

- **Constancy of experience.** Because the body changes slowly, most people maintain what psychologists call *constancy of experience*—they still feel like their "old self." Our sense of self doesn't change much as we age, and even in our 70s and 80s, many of us carry around a mental image of ourselves as being younger and more vigorous than we really are. Ball fields and dance floors are strewn with the ailing bodies of women and men who thought they could still toss the football a mile, or shake their booty like they did back in high school. (Message to all you aging dancers who threw your back out doing the hustle at your nephew's wedding: disco is dead—move on. Please.)

- **Denial.** Contrary to popular belief, denial isn't always a bad thing. When asked to make judgments about our health, most of us show what researchers call "self-serving bias": we expect to live longer, healthier lives than the average person our age. Our self-serving bias protects us from ruminating obsessively about our health and mortality, and a bit of denial (just a bit, not too much) actually motivates us to engage in health-promoting behaviors like watching our diet and exercising regularly. Studies even suggest that denial can be helpful when confronted with bad news: upon learning that they have a serious disease, those adults who convince themselves that they'll be among the select few who'll recover adhere more conscientiously to treatment regimens—and fare better in the long run as a result.

- **Accommodation.** It's a subtle process, and often goes unnoticed, but consciously or unconsciously most of us slowly tweak our behavior to accommodate the realities of aging. Bikinis give way to one-piece suits, runners become walkers, tennis pros become commentators who share their wisdom regarding the game. We're surprisingly good at tailoring our behavior to accommodate our evolving abilities, which enables us to enjoy many of the things we've always enjoyed, but from a different perspective.

Physicians, scientists, and philosophers don't always agree, but here the consensus is clear. The mind is a wonderful thing—it can smooth life's rough edges, and enable us to store, retrieve, and process the information we need to function well (if not always gracefully), despite the inroads of time.

Staying Active

If you've ever been hospitalized for surgery, you might have wondered why the nurses and aides were so adamant about getting you up on your feet as soon as possible, trudging up and down the hall with your IV pole. The short answer is their fear of "deconditioning." If you stay in bed without moving much for a few days, you'll show signs of serious muscle atrophy, even if you're in peak physical condition. Extend your stay in bed past two weeks and your skin may start to break down ("bedsores"), and your sense of balance will begin to skew (you actually have to "practice" balance or you lose it). You'll also experience an overpowering feeling of fatigue and muscle weakness. After a few weeks off your feet, you might literally have to learn to walk all over again—a process far less pleasant the second time around.

ADAPTING EXERCISE REGIMENS TO LATER LIFE

Some people can continue doing what they did in their 20s throughout their lives, not missing a beat along the way. Most televised marathons feature an 80-something runner who began training at 60, and feel-good evening news stories celebrate the oldest-ever Mt. Everest climber or English Channel swimmer. These achievements are laudable, but they are also statistically unusual—most of us simply aren't built to do these things. Insistence on trying will almost certainly lead to injury, or worse (many televised marathons also feature stories about runners who succumbed to heart attacks during the race).

For most of us, staying active throughout our retirement years requires that we alter our routine to fit our current skill and fitness level. These three strategies help:

- **Dial it back.** Those of us raised in the era of "no pain, no gain" often believe that a workout isn't any good unless it makes you suffer. In fact, considerable data suggest that gentler movement may be almost as effective in terms of health benefits, while being much easier on the body. Walking won't get your heart pumping as fast as running on a treadmill, but if you keep it up longer, the cardiovascular and pulmonary benefits are still great. Tai chi offers a low-stress alternative to more vigorous martial arts.

- **Pace yourself.** Coaxing your body into motion takes a little longer with age, and the importance of proper warm-ups and stretching before springing into action is more important now than ever before. Making sure that you're ready to progress from the initial phase of an activity to the more strenuous stage is also crucial in avoiding injury. A workout may take a little longer at 60 than it did at 40, and you'll probably have to spend more time ramping up to full speed, but it's worth it.

- **Portion control.** Some studies suggest that briefer, more frequent workouts yield better health results than fewer workouts of longer duration. They also increase the likelihood that you'll actually stay on track: it's easier to free up several fifteen- or twenty-minute time blocks in the course of a day than a whole unbroken hour. (One of us uses this approach himself, taking three twenty-minute walks around campus each day, rain or shine.)

TO GYM, OR NOT TO GYM?

For some of us, exercise isn't really exercise unless it takes place in a gym. For others, the very idea of hanging out with "gym rats" is aversive. (Count the two of us, nonathletes with bad memories of high school gym class, among that group.) Putting aside one's stereotypes and traumatic teenage years, there are pros and cons to both approaches.

>> STEALTH EXERCISE

Some years ago people became obsessed with building little exercise "extras" into their daily routines. A small cottage industry grew up around this, and for a while it seemed as though everyone was wearing a pedometer, tracking their mileage and trying to add a few thousand steps to their day. Never having had much luck getting pedometers to work properly, we suspect that frustration with the technology may have contributed to the demise of that particular movement. (Our smartphones now promise to become foolproof pedometers if we download the proper app, but we're skeptical.)

Technological glitches notwithstanding, the concept is sound: building extra movement into your daily routine won't make you into an Olympian, but it really does help. So try:

- Taking stairs instead of elevators
- Deliberately choosing parking spaces further from your destination
- Taking the long way to your destination rather than the most efficient path
- Making more trips to put away groceries or laundry (also better for your back)

The bottom line: Much of what we do is exercise—we just don't think of it that way. Scrubbing the floor, mowing the lawn, bending and stretching to wash down the shower stall tiles—all involve activity, and all burn calories. Ditto for raking leaves, washing cars, hauling trash cans, walking to work—you name it. (You can use the worksheet on page 219 to calculate how many calories you burn each day doing tasks you'd likely carry out anyway, and to increase the number of calories you burn by adding in additional activities here and there.)

THE ADVANTAGES OF GYMS

- **Structure.** Gyms have the equipment that will help you meet your goals. Machines are calibrated to guide you through specific, planned increases in difficulty levels, allowing you to track your progress more effectively. Routines and classes are designed to work specific muscle groups, in sequences that optimize results. Many of us need the external structure of a gym—we're less likely to slack off or skip steps if there's a clear path to follow, and periodic progress reports.

- **Commitment.** For some, the idea of not wasting money is very motivating. Given the substantial costs of a gym membership, the idea that you'll "lose your money" if you don't use the service can be compelling. Once you develop connections with people at the facility, staff as well as other members, this can provide a bit of extra incentive as well. (They'll comment if you disappear for a while.)

- **Guidance and support.** Most gyms have instructors who offer suggestions and advice (though sometimes there's an additional fee for this). Instructors' input can help prevent injuries (many novices tend to take on too much too fast), and it may be motivating as well, if it includes the occasional compliment, and recognition of your efforts.

So those are the advantages of a gym. These advantages are crucial for some, less important for others.

THE ADVANTAGES OF EXERCISING ON YOUR OWN

- **Privacy.** Exercising on your own is private. Many of us aren't enthusiastic about being seen in workout togs, and let's face it: exercise isn't always pretty. If the path to health and beauty passes through a sweaty, jiggly dance routine involving sweats and an old, ripped tee shirt, you might prefer to keep that particular image to yourself. And unless you attend an age-targeted gym (they do exist), or figure out the hours when the older folks are there, you may find yourself surrounded by a sea of buff 20-somethings—nice scenery, but not always good for the ego.

- **No (or low) cost.** Gym membership isn't cheap—and don't be fooled by the low introductory rates, which escalate considerably after the first few months. Studies show that nearly half of those who join gyms stop going within a year (New Year's resolutions notwithstanding). If you think you might be one of those well-intentioned quitters, you may not want to devote your resources to something you won't follow through on. Exercising on your own is virtually free (unless you purchase home workout equipment, but that's a one-time thing). The American Senior Fitness Association provides good information in this area; you can visit their website at www.seniorfitness.net. Or check out Sit and Be Fit with Mary Ann Wilson, a nonprofit organization devoted to fitness and healthy aging at www.sitandbefit.org (many PBS stations carry this program as well—check your local listings).

- **Time and place—your choice.** To the degree that your exercise routines are "portable," you'll be more likely to stay with them, which is particularly important if you travel frequently. If you opt for a gym, you're constrained by location and hours; plus, there's travel time. While some urban venues offer twenty-four-hour convenience, that's not as common in suburban and rural areas, so if you want to work out at midnight or 5 a.m., you're out of luck.

Managing Stress

In 1956, cardiologist Meyer Friedman made a chance observation that changed the course of medical history. While having his waiting room furniture reupholstered, he noticed that the cloth on the chairs was worn away up front (not toward the back, as usual), as if his patients had been perched on the edge of their seats, waiting anxiously to be called by the receptionist. That's odd, thought Dr. Friedman; it's as though all my patients feel pressured and stressed, anxious to get in and get done with their appointment.

The Type A personality was born.

And Dr. Friedman was right: decades of research confirms that stress harms us—it increases our risk for heart disease, and for other serious illnesses (like cancer). Monitoring and managing stress will not only help you feel better, it will also help you live longer.

THE HUMAN STRESS RESPONSE

Here are three principles to keep in mind to cope effectively with stress:

- **Stress doesn't happen to you, it happens within you.** Most people equate stress with negative events (like arguing with your partner or getting yelled at by your boss), but that's not really accurate. Stress happens within us—it's the body's reflexive reaction to potential threats (the well-known "fight or flight" response). So stress isn't losing your keys, it's the increase in heart rate, breathing, and blood pressure that occur when you discover that your keys are nowhere to be found (along with the frustration you feel).

- **Positive as well as negative events can be stressful.** Health researchers distinguish *distress* (stress that follows negative events) from *eustress* (stress that follows positive events). We know, it seems strange, but eustress is actually as harmful as distress. Getting a new job can be as stressful as getting fired from your old one (since both create uncertainty, and require you to adapt). Getting married can be as stressful as getting divorced. (Well, anyone who has tried to plan a wedding surrounded by kvetchy, intrusive family members knows that!)

- **Endless minor hassles may be worse than significant negative events.** It's counterintuitive, but true: an unending series of minor annoyances—they really are called "hassles" by researchers—can be more destructive than a smaller number of more serious problems. Being involved in a fender-bender is a significant stressor, but it happens, it's over, and you move on. Missing the bus, getting soaked in the rain, watching the elevator doors close in your face, and spilling your coffee as you rush down the hallway to make it to work on time are all minor things, but collectively they tax the body terribly because each negative event causes your blood pressure and heart rate to soar, after which you must expend energy to bring things back to normal. And then the sequence repeats itself. It's the repetition—one upset close on the heels of another—that's so destructive.

The flip side of hassles is uplifts—those seemingly minor positive events (like getting a compliment) that lift our mood and make our day. We've talked about the negative impact that hassles can have when they accumulate, piling one atop the other. You can't avoid hassles (sometimes you miss the bus—it happens), but you can minimize hassles' negative effects by countering them with uplifts.

Some uplifts (like finding a dollar) are beyond our control; others we create ourselves. So when you're feeling down, take charge and create your own uplifts. Here are some things you can do:

- Compliment a colleague, friend, or stranger
- Hold the door for someone
- Let another driver go first
- Invite someone who's in a hurry to get in front of you in line
- Give up your seat on the bus
- Pet a dog or a neighborhood cat
- Retrieve your neighbor's empty trash can and set it back in place

You might think of other, better ways to create uplifts in your day, but however you do it, the process is the same: when you act in ways that make others feel better, you'll feel better as well.

COPING WITH STRESS

Understanding stress is one thing; coping is another. Six strategies are especially effective. The first two involve other people; the other four you can do on your own:

- **Social support.** The findings are clear: people who lean on others in times of stress fare better than those who go it alone. We call this *healthy dependency*, and it's an extraordinarily powerful coping strategy (more on that in chapter 9). For now, consider this: illness and mortality rates are 30 percent lower in widows and widowers who get support from others than those who try to cope on their own. Cancer patients who have high levels of social support live significantly longer than socially isolated patients, and they experience less pain and anxiety.

- **Unburdening.** Twenty years ago psychologist James Pennebaker made a surprising discovery: talking to others about things that upset you actually enhances immune system function and lowers illness rates. Pennebaker's findings have been replicated many times, and it's clear that unburdening yourself is good for you. It doesn't matter whether you talk face to face, over the phone, or even via Skype or email—if something's bugging you, tell someone about it. You'll feel better, and function better, too.

- **Exercise.** We discussed the health benefits of exercise in the previous section. *Aerobic exercise* (exercise that raises your heart and breathing rate) has stress-reducing effects as well. Exercise causes the brain to release mood-enhancing neurotransmitters called endorphins, and it boosts cognitive function by increasing blood flow to the brain. So find a way to build regular exercise into your schedule—at least a couple of hours each week. (But always check with your physician before beginning a new exercise regimen.)

- **Meditation.** When we were young, such things were considered "fringe," but meditation has gone mainstream: the National Institutes of Health actually has an entire division devoted to alternative medicine, which funds research on the health benefits of meditation. When you're feeling overwhelmed, try to find a quiet space where you can relax, focus on the moment, and clear your mind. If you make time for meditation every day, or a few times each week, you'll help prevent minor hassles from overwhelming you. Twenty minutes should do it. (If you're busy, ten minutes is fine.)

- **Reframing.** It's easy to let minor problems snowball in your mind and take on greater importance than they deserve; psychologists call this *magnification*. Here a bit of reframing can be a great help. If you're bothered by the fact that your brother-in-law has more money than you

>> THE HEALING POWER OF PETS

If you've ever been pounced on by a retriever when you walked in the door, or been cozied up to by a tabby while you lay on the couch, you know: pets provide unconditional love. Several decades of research confirms that Fido and Fluffy provide way more than that. They actually help stave off illness and speed recovery if illness occurs. Consider this:

- **Cats and dogs control blood pressure better than medications do.** While medications are often effective in controlling hypertension, they don't moderate stress-related spikes in blood pressure as well as the presence of a dog or cat. Preliminary evidence from long-term studies suggests that adopting a dog or cat may also be associated with less plaque buildup in arteries and lower risk of heart disease.

- **Pets provide exercise.** Okay, we're talking mainly about dogs here (ever try to walk a cat?), but the evidence is clear: people with pets spend more time walking each week than their pet-deprived counterparts, especially in urban areas. (Plus, trying to get a cat to take a pill is exercise—sort of—if you count hand-to-paw combat as exercise.)

- **Pets have calming effects.** Studies show that petting a dog or cat (or hamster or ferret) can reduce anxiety and brighten your mood. Among people with chronic diseases (like debilitating arthritis), those with pets report less depression than those without. Heart attack survivors with pets actually live longer than those who don't have pets. Regardless of whether they're at home or in a skilled care facility, people with dementia become less agitated when a furry companion is close at hand.

- **Dogs are date magnets, especially for shy people.** Walking a dog can become a social event, especially if your pooch is friendly. People who would never think of approaching a stranger on the street don't hesitate to walk right up to dog owners and start chatting.

do, focus instead on all the comforts that you do have (not those you don't). If you're scheduled to undergo laser surgery to correct glaucoma, don't dwell on the misfortune of being ill, but on the miracle of medicine that will enable you to be treated quickly and effectively. (Think about how grateful your grandparents would have been to have such an opportunity available to them when their vision declined.)

- **Distraction.** It seems simple, but it works: if you're feeling overwhelmed, do something to distract yourself from the problems at hand. Go shopping, see a movie, visit with friends, or take a spa day. Getting your mind off your troubles—switching gears—can go a long way toward reducing stress. (That's why people usually return from a vacation feeling recharged and refreshed: even if the trip itself was just okay, being away from your routine provides distraction, a change of scene, and time off from ruminating about everyday worries.)

The bottom line: You can't eliminate stress, but you can control how you respond to life's ups and downs. Whether you encounter minor hassles or major upsets, stress need not rule your life.

Eat to Live

We met on the first day of graduate school at SUNY–Buffalo, on September 1, 1981, at the orientation for incoming clinical psychology doctoral students. Within a year, we had moved in together (though it took us another decade to get married—apparently we don't like to rush into things).

Back then we spent many a Saturday night at home, sharing a pizza with the works and two dozen Buffalo wings, the whole mess washed down by a couple of liters of sugary cola. Never one to quit easily, Bob would often end the evening by downing a few pickles from the fridge, just to take the edge off. (That cola was awfully sweet.)

Those were the days. . .

As we age, gastric acidity changes, intestinal motility slows, kidneys lose some of their filtering power, and insulin may fail to do its job as effectively as it once did. As a result, you'll probably be more prone to indigestion, reflux, nausea, constipation, and a host of other digestive woes. You may find that you can no longer tolerate the spicy foods you once loved (we can't, unfortunately—no more wings for us). Your physician may tell you to lay off the sweets and carbs. The martini that once produced a pleasant buzz now makes you dizzy.

Does this mean your days of enjoying food and drink are over? No—as long as you use your head. Portion size, intensity of spice or heat, and the contents of your cocktail can all be tweaked. You can pace yourself, eating smaller portions more slowly. (Do you *really* need an entire turkey leg? A foot-long sub? A six pack?) Preventive medications are available to quell some of the impact of Szechuan or Thai food. Many ingredients have healthy substitutes that taste pretty close to the originals.

A few simple strategies can lead to healthier eating (not to mention a better night's sleep afterward). Let's look at these now.

THE COMPANY WE KEEP

People who eat with others eat better. Older adults who live alone sometimes lose weight because they skip meals; others gain weight because they subsist on a steady diet of toaster waffles and junk food. Maybe it's the distraction of conversation, or the need to watch your table manners, but whatever it is, mealtime companionship usually translates into better nutrition. This is one reason that shared prepared meals at senior centers and other group venues tend to result in better health for the participants.

PESKY CALORIES

Because 3,500 calories translates into one pound of fat, you need to burn that many extra calories to lose a pound. It's not as bad as it sounds, because you don't have to do it all at once. (In fact, slower is better where weight loss is concerned.) If you burn an extra 100 calories per day (or reduce your daily calorie intake by 100, or any combination of the two), you could lose about a pound per month. That's twelve pounds in a year. We include a Calories Burned Worksheet on page 219; if you're watching your weight, you can use this worksheet to keep a record of your activities and the approximate number of calories burned by each.

TOGETHER WE STAND

Food prices are going up—not news. This is why "couponing" is now a verb, and more people are taking advantage of big box stores and buying clubs that sell food and other items in bulk at lower prices. (Some involve an annual membership fee, but if you use them fairly often, it's worth it.) One good option is to shop with friends, splitting the costs and dividing up the mega-size portions.

COOKING FOR ONE (OR TWO)

If you're accustomed to preparing meals for a gang, the work involved in cooking for one (or even two) people may strike you as a "why bother?" experience. It needn't be. You can still prepare a big pot of stew—you'll just freeze some portions for later. Cooking for one or two allows you the luxury of creating simpler and more elegant meals, and indulging the occasional culinary experiment. After decades of trying to please a crowd, it can be fun to eat what you want.

MEAL CLUBS AND COOPERATIVES

Just as shopping opportunities can be shared, so can the meals themselves. If you buy meat in bulk, try splitting it with neighbors, each preparing your specialty then swapping the dishes among yourselves. You'll get savings, variety, and the chance to benefit from others' culinary mastery. Some people opt to share the food literally, dining together and making an event of it—now you get company as well as good food.

And there you have it: Good self-care is key to successful aging in place. It can help you live the life you want, where you want, maximizing your health and wellness for as long as possible. A positive attitude, adequate exercise, effective coping skills, and healthy diet won't guarantee happiness, but they sure can help.

>> ALCOHOL AND DRUGS

Stereotypes notwithstanding, drug abuse is a serious and growing problem among older adults. About 17 percent of people 65+ have a substance abuse problem. In many cases, late-life substance abuse involves prescription drugs or alcohol (or both in combination), but increasingly it centers around recreational drugs from our youth, especially marijuana. Oftentimes late-life drug use simply reflects a lifetime pattern that's continuing through another phase; in some cases, it's a problem that onsets for the first time post-retirement (for example, when use of a pain medication spirals out of control, or alcohol use increases because the person is isolated and has little else to do).

Here are a few things to keep in mind to prevent social drinking or moderate drug use from becoming a problem:

- As we discussed earlier in the chapter with respect to prescription and over-the-counter medications, the aging body metabolizes mood-altering drugs more slowly than the younger body; it takes less now to get the desired effect.

- Women are not immune from late-life substance abuse. Quite the opposite, in fact: although a greater proportion of older men than older women have substance use problems, more women than men begin drinking heavily later in life.

- Losses often precipitate substance abuse, as people drink or drug to self-medicate and "take the edge off" their feelings of upset. Death of a loved one and bad health news are common precipitants of late-life substance abuse. Retirement is as well (because retired people have more time on their hands).

- Treatment programs developed for younger adults are often ineffective for older adults, who have different concerns, conflicts, norms, and experiences. If at some point you decide you need help, ask your physician to refer you to a treatment program tailored to people in your age group.

CHAPTER 8

Healthy Spirit

Some years ago, Nobel Prize–winner Elie Wiesel spoke at a college near our home. He described the terrible things he'd witnessed during the Holocaust, and he spoke at length about ongoing inhumanities and injustices taking place around the world.

It was a powerful speech, and when Mr. Wiesel finished, there was a long silence. Finally, a student raised her hand and asked, "What can be done? What can I do to make a difference?" Mr. Wiesel paused, reflected, and finally responded, "Pick up a shovel, and start where you stand."

Terrible things happen—tragic things. The world is not always a happy place. We can choose to remain angry about injustices and lost opportunities, or—like Mr. Wiesel—we can choose to move forward. That's what this chapter is about.

Adulthood Is a Time of Growth and Change

Sigmund Freud once wrote that there was no point in doing psychotherapy with anyone over 40 because by that age one's habits are set in stone—it's too late to change. In Freud's view, psychological growth and development occur rapidly throughout childhood, slow during adolescence, and are pretty much done by the time you reach your 20s.

Boy, did Freud have that one wrong.

The psychoanalyst Erik Erikson had a different, more accurate take on things. In Erikson's view, growth occurs throughout life. From early childhood through old age, we are never static, ever-changing.

According to Erikson's "life stage" model, we go through a series of challenges (he called them *psychosocial crises*) at different ages, each challenge reflecting the major issues we must confront during that phase of life. In infancy, our primary task is to gain a sense of *basic trust*—a belief that the world is a safe and nurturing place. As we begin to move about on our own (first crawling, then walking), our sense of *autonomy* is shaped; we gain confidence in our ability to navigate a complex world. A bit later our feelings about taking *initiative* are formed: are our creative efforts valued, or criticized?

In school, we confront conflicts around competence (what Erikson called *industry*): do our products measure up to those of our peers—can we hold our own and compete? And adolescence brings with it uncertainties about our *identity*. It's a crucial time, often fraught with self-doubt; most of us remember this period vividly. Though not set in stone (Freud was wrong indeed), it is during the adolescent years that we make significant choices about who we are and what we want to do with our life.

> There are life stages unique to adulthood—challenges we're not prepared to confront until we're 50, 60, or 70. The great thing about these challenges is that each presents an opportunity to reinvent ourselves— a chance to rethink old assumptions, revise old habits, and try new things.

Identity, it seems, is more complex than even Erikson thought. Not only must we create our identity in multiple domains (sexuality, career, personal philosophy, political beliefs), but it turns out that adolescence is just the start. Our identities evolve throughout adulthood, as liberal leanings morph into conservative ideals (or vice versa), and circumstances prompt us to question our career choices, life goals—even our sexual orientation.

And even then we're not complete: as Erikson pointed out, there are life stages unique to adulthood—challenges we're not prepared to confront until we're 50, 60, or 70. The great thing about these challenges is that each presents

>> FORGIVENESS

On October 2, 2006, Charles Carl Roberts took over a schoolhouse in the Old Order Amish community of Nickel Mines, Pennsylvania. He shot ten young girls, killing five, before committing suicide. It was a terrible, tragic event, and many of us remember the extensive news coverage. What many of us may not remember is the response of the Amish community.

They forgave Charles Roberts—immediately, completely, and without reservation. The evening of the shootings—the very same day—representatives of the Amish community visited with Roberts's widow and parents, comforting them and offering support. They brought food to Roberts's family to help them in their hour of grief. About thirty members of the Amish community attended Charles Roberts's funeral. They eventually set up a charitable fund for Roberts's wife and children. As one member of the community noted, "I don't think there's anybody here that wants to do anything but forgive . . . and reach out to the family of the man who committed these acts."

Most of us have been wronged by someone at some point in our life—whether it was casual or malicious, intentional or inadvertent. The romantic partner who cheated on us, the friend who convinced us to invest in the "next big thing," the grade school mentor, teacher, or coach

an opportunity to reinvent ourselves—a chance to rethink old assumptions, revise old habits, and try new things. Three stages—intimacy, generativity, integrity—provide a road map for our journey through adulthood:

INTIMACY

Although Erikson saw intimacy as a task of adolescence, recent research suggests that intimacy evolves long beyond our teenage years, deepening as we age and gain experience and perspective. If you think back, you may be able to see this in yourself: the intimacies of adolescence—though powerful at the time—are quite different from the intimacies we experience later in life, when our commitments are deeper, and shared values and goals take on increasing importance.

who took advantage of our vulnerability and violated our trust. Hurts linger, and it's not uncommon to feel angry and resentful for years—even decades—after the event. Anyone who has experienced this sort of hurt won't be surprised to learn that such festering anger and resentment can have lasting negative effects, impairing our health and destroying friendships and family ties (more on this latter issue in chapter 9).

Sometimes it's not possible to confront the person who wronged us—and sometimes it's simply not helpful to do so. But as the Amish community showed us, there's another, better option.

When you forgive someone who has hurt you, you make a conscious choice to put the matter to rest. You let go of resentment and the urge to seek revenge, no matter how deserving of these things the person may be. Fault and blame are not the issues here; the goal of forgiveness is allowing yourself to move beyond the hurt.

Although forgiveness was once a topic reserved for philosophy and religion, in recent years a number of research studies have examined the positive effects of forgiving past slights—and there are many. Some are physical (lower blood pressure, improved immune function), some are psychological (increased optimism, decreased depression), but the most important positive effect of forgiveness is also the simplest: peace of mind.

GENERATIVITY

We all want to be remembered—to leave our mark on the world—and one way we do this is by creating things that symbolize who we are, things that will be here to represent us after we're gone. Many people fulfill their generativity needs by having children—what better way to leave behind a part of oneself? For others, generativity means painting a masterpiece or writing a great novel; others teach, mentor, or do charitable work.

INTEGRITY

As we move through our 60s and 70s, issues regarding mortality become more prominent in our minds. As we reflect on what we've accomplished so far, we ask ourselves: have I spent my time well and made a positive impact on the world? In Erikson's view, satisfaction with the answers to those questions can imbue our final years with a deep sense of integrity and fulfillment. Otherwise, our poor choices may come back to haunt us one last time, and we experience regret and despair.

>> DEALING WITH STEREOTYPE AND PREJUDICE: AGEISM

We all experience it at one time or another: having classified us as "old," people (even well-meaning people) unintentionally—often unconsciously—begin to treat us as if we're slow, frail, and forgetful. That's how ageism works: it's rarely deliberate, but more often operates automatically, reflexively, and with minimal conscious awareness.

Keep in mind that ageism isn't limited to young people—older adults hold ageist attitudes and beliefs as well. How can we get past ageism (including our own)? Here are several things to do:

- **Obtain accurate information about aging.** The National Institute on Aging (www.nih.gov/nia) is a great source for accurate, up-to-date information on healthy aging and age-related challenges.

- **Confront ageist stereotypes.** They're pervasive, and once they take hold, they're hard to undo. Misperceptions notwithstanding, dementia is relatively rare, even among the very old, but hardly anyone thinks of it that way.

- **Speak up and speak out.** When you see ageism in a magazine article or news program, say something. Email, blog, tweet, or write a letter to the editor.

- **Support organizations that address ageism.** The AARP is an obvious choice, but there are others as well. The American Psychological Association has been active in combating ageism in recent years (www.apa.org); the Health and Age website (www.healthandage.org) is another good resource.

- **Connect with elected officials.** Older adults are politically engaged—they go to the polls and vote. Elected officials know that, and they take our opinions seriously.

Unfinished Business

At this point, you might be thinking, all right, that's interesting, but why the mini-course in adult development? The take-home message here is, many of us still have unfinished business, even later in life. Erikson's work points us toward some of the key challenges of adulthood and opportunities to address them in new ways. If there are aspects of your most important relationships that seem unsettled to you, now is the time to deal with them. Now is the time to paint that painting or write that novel. It's time to think seriously about your legacy as well—how you want to be remembered after you're gone, which brings us to an uncomfortable but unavoidable topic.

THE D WORD

We humans are not good at thinking realistically about death. It's too frightening. So we speak about dying in euphemism ("he's no longer with us," "she's in a better place"), and we distance ourselves from the reality of death. (Few people die at home anymore; instead we spend our last days in a hospital.) Most religions offer elaborate explanations of what happens to us after we die—heaven, hell, reincarnation—and despite their differences, these explanations share a common theme: religion assures us that even after we die, we still exist in some form.

We're not knocking religion here—not at all—but from a scientific standpoint these common themes tell us something important about ourselves: it's easier to ponder our own mortality if we think of death as a transition to another place (heaven, hell, reincarnation) than if we think of death as a final ending, the permanent shutting down of consciousness. Pulitzer Prize–winning author Ernest Becker put it well when he wrote: "The idea of death . . . haunts the human animal like nothing else; it is a mainspring of human activity—activity designed largely to avoid the fatality of death, to overcome it by denying in some way that it is the final destiny for man."

Not a pleasant topic—we get that—but it's important, so let's push on.

>> DEALING WITH YOUR OWN PREJUDICES

Here's an uncomfortable fact: no matter how open-minded we are, we all hold stereotypes regarding gender, ethnicity, and other human characteristics. Yup—it's true; studies confirm it. Researchers from Harvard, Yale, the University of Washington, and elsewhere have found that when we encounter an unfamiliar person, we reflexively attribute characteristics to that person based on easily identifiable attributes like age and ethnicity. If you don't believe it, try it yourself, by taking a quick test on Harvard's "Project Implicit" website: https://implicit.harvard.edu/implicit (or just Google "Harvard Project Implicit"). But be forewarned: you might not like what you find.

We all stereotype, but that doesn't make us bad people. Stereotypes result from the fact that humans are *cognitive misers*: we don't like to spend more mental energy than we have to when dealing with the unfamiliar. So we use shortcuts (psychologists call them *heuristics*), and draw quick inferences regarding people based on surface characteristics. Over time, as we get to know people as individuals, we overcome our initial reaction and see them as they are—as unique individuals, not merely a representative of a particular group.

So what can you do? Several things:

- Be mindful of your prejudices. You have them—we all do—but knowing that they exist is the first step in overcoming them.

- Understand that prejudices and stereotypes tend to emerge most when we feel threatened. After 9/11, even open-minded people found themselves harboring secret, shameful thoughts about what "those people" did to us (and what we should do to them in response).

- Contact is key. Study after study confirms that one of the best ways to overcome prejudice is to have personal contact with people from diverse backgrounds and different life experiences. It's harder to maintain biases when you truly know a person.

A SOLUTION

It's ironic, but true: the way to move beyond our fear of death is not to avoid it or fight it off, but to embrace it. We must accept the fact that our time on earth is limited, and therefore precious. We must make mindful choices about how we want to spend our retirement years rather than drifting mindlessly along our old, familiar path without thinking about what we'd really like to accomplish in the time we have remaining.

Making mindful choices is not always easy (more on that in a bit), but there's a strategy you can use to focus your attention on what's really important and move beyond the distractions of the day. When you feel yourself drifting along, wasting time on things that you'd rather not be doing, ask yourself: If I knew for sure that this was my last day on earth, how would I want to spend it? If I had only twenty-four hours left, would I still choose to do what I'm doing right now?

These are powerful questions. Asking them will make you mindful of the difference between what you are doing out of habit and what you truly want to do. Now you have a choice to make—and that choice is up to you.

Finding Your Bliss: If Not Now, When?

Developing an awareness of how we want to spend our time post-retirement is just the start. The opportunities are many, and decisions must be made. You know best what experiences would be most meaningful to you; here are two possibilities: travel and exploration, and spirituality and religion.

TRAVEL AND EXPLORATION

Most of us believe that our experience of the world is close to the norm— that everyone sees things the way we do. That's why travel can be such a powerful experience: being "a stranger in a strange land" really is transformative. There's something about finding yourself in a new world, surrounded by unfamiliar customs and language, food and dress that is both unsettling and liberating. If you want to connect with the experiences that really matter—those bedrock things that make us all human—there's nothing like experiencing firsthand the common bonds we share with others. And if you do, you're likely to discover something unexpected, but reassuring as well: although there are tremendous differences in how people from different cultures experience themselves and the world, when you focus in on the important things—family and friends, hopes and fears—in the end, we're all pretty much the same.

One of us has done quite a bit of therapy with folks immersed in end-of-life reflection, and here the importance of travel and exploration becomes clear: as people look back on how they spent their time—what experiences they valued most—travel memories bubble up again and again. For many of us, these represent life's "high points"—life's most transcendent moments. Although people often regret having worked too much, or having spent too much time doing things they didn't really like, we've yet to meet someone who regretted the time they spent traveling and exploring themselves and the world. (We provided links to some good travel websites in our Tours and Getaways sidebar on page 86; you can find additional options in the Resource and Contact Information section on page 242.)

> Retirement is an ideal time to do some essential self-examination, and to get in touch with what you truly believe (and why). Some people find that organized religion helps with this process; others follow a more unique and personal path, not tethered to any established school of thought.

SPIRITUALITY AND RELIGION

Descartes argued that a willingness to question one's beliefs is crucial to developing a personal philosophy. True faith—genuine commitment—requires that we actively consider the possibility that our way of thinking might, in fact, be wrong. This sort of challenging, pondering, and questioning is most meaningful when it comes from within.

Retirement is an ideal time to do some essential self-examination, and to get in touch with what you truly believe (and why). Some people find that organized religion helps with this process; others follow a more unique and personal path, not tethered to any established school of thought. For many of us quiet contemplation is helpful as well; others find that doing is more helpful than thinking, and that devoting time and energy to good works is most important. Service to others lets us experience the joy of sharing our wisdom, the insight that comes from putting our beliefs to the test, and the deepened perspective that comes from hands-on experience.

>> SPIRITUALITY AND HEALTH

Once considered to be on the fringes of medical science, research on spirituality and health has gone mainstream: a tremendous amount of supportive evidence has accumulated during the past several decades, and the National Institutes of Health now funds research on the links between spirituality and health through their Center for Complementary and Alternative Medicine.

The findings are compelling. For example, studies show that people who attend religious services regularly have healthier immune systems than those who don't, and lower blood pressure as well. Cardiac surgery patients with strong religious ties have higher survival rates than those who don't have strong spiritual connections. One long-term study found that over the course of nearly a decade, older adults with the greatest amount of religious involvement showed less depression and fewer illness episodes than similar adults who were not as religious.

So we know that spirituality is associated with better health, but the question remains: what's the link? Three factors play a role:

- Spirituality helps people cope with life's challenges through faith; it gives purpose to life and meaning to challenge, setback, and loss.
- Religious people have better social support—they have a broader network of people they can turn to in times of trouble.
- Prayer itself seems to have health-promoting effects: like meditation, prayer decreases blood pressure, lowers heart rate, and enhances immune function.

>> HOSPICE

Like so many aspects of death and dying, hospice is frequently misunderstood. Certain myths and misperceptions surround hospice care, but you should know the facts.

What Is Hospice?

Hospice is a loosely knit organization of caregivers—doctors, nurses, psychologists, social workers, clergy, and others—who share a single, simple view: that death is a normal part of life. Hospice workers strive to make the dying person's final days as dignified, fulfilling, and comfortable as possible by using *palliative care* (sometimes called *comfort care*). Hospice workers are trained in recognizing and managing pain, and skilled at managing the unpleasant symptoms of fatal illness in its latter stages.

Note that hospice is *not* assisted suicide. (That's a myth.) Hospice workers do not hasten death deliberately or encourage people to "pull the plug." Although many hospice workers oppose aggressive end-of-life medical treatments or invasive life support, they work with patients and their families to find care options that enhance whatever life the person chooses.

Who Is Eligible for Hospice?

To become eligible for hospice, an attending physician must certify that the person is terminally ill—that he or she has six months or less to live. Because physicians hesitate to declare a person terminally ill, most people actually have less than six months left by the time they are declared hospice eligible. If the physician's prognosis turns out to be wrong, and the patient's condition stabilizes or improves, they can be discharged from hospice and returned to other levels of care. (That actually happens more than you might think.)

Who Pays for the Service?

Hospice is unique—it is the only form of custodial care funded by Medicare. Once a physician declares a person hospice eligible, Medicare will pay for two ninety-day periods and an unlimited number of sixty-day periods in a Medicare-approved hospice program. This arrangement allows a person to be discharged from hospice then readmitted later—as many times as needed.

Now you know the facts. You can obtain more detailed information regarding hospice philosophies and services from three national organizations:

American Academy of Hospice and Palliative Medicine
4700 West Lake Drive
Glenview, IL 60025
847-375-4712
info@aahpm.org
www.aahpm.org

Hospice Foundation of America
1710 Rhode Island Avenue, NW
Suite 400
Washington, DC 20036
202-457-5811
800-854-3402
hfaoffice@hospicefoundation.org
www.hospicefoundation.org

Compassion & Choices
PO Box 101810
Denver, CO 80250
800-247-7421
www.compassionandchoices.org

Healthy Mind, Healthy Spirit

In chapter 6, we discussed the benefits of a healthy mind—the ways you can nurture your cognitive skills to make your retirement years as good as they can be. Here's an opportunity: you can use your healthy mind to nurture a healthy spirit. Two strategies are especially helpful—mindfulness and optimism.

MINDFULNESS: LIVING IN THE MOMENT

Mindfulness is awareness of the present—the here and now. It involves bringing your attention to present experience so you become fully aware of each thought, feeling, and sensation that enters your consciousness. A key feature of mindfulness is acceptance: you attend to each experience as it occurs, without judgment.

It sounds simple, but it isn't. Many of us find it hard to focus on present experience—our mind drifts back to the past (Did I leave the coffee maker on?), or ahead toward the future (I'd better confirm that appointment. . .). And many of us, meaning well, try too hard: instead of allowing the moment to come to us, we concentrate on screening out competing thoughts. Such focused concentration prevents us from experiencing things in the here and now, and the moment is lost.

Mindfulness isn't something one can acquire by brute force—for some people it comes fairly easily; for others, it's more of a challenge—but there are things we can do to practice mindfulness and come closer to achieving it. Like many things in life, it's the journey toward mindfulness that's most important.

Here's an exercise to get you started; it's called "One Minute of Mindfulness." You begin by checking your watch; for the next sixty seconds, your task is to focus on your breathing. Leave your eyes open, but don't gaze at anything in particular. Breathe normally, and allow yourself to experience each breath as it enters, and then as it leaves when you exhale. If your mind begins to wander (it probably will the first few times you try this) just bring it back to the moment, focus on your breathing, and finish your mindfulness minute.

>> THE MIND OF A CHILD

In some ways, practicing mindfulness is like trying to recapture the experience of being a child. To children, every experience is fresh and every sensation new. As adults, we become jaded and forget this, but it's possible to recapture that childlike sense of wonder. Four exercises—mindful observation, body awareness, mindful listening, mindful eating—can help.

Mindful Observation

Choose an object (a pen, a vase, a pillow—it doesn't matter) and gaze at it for one minute. Appreciate its uniqueness—its size, shape, contour, color—whatever captures your interest. Try not to overthink things—there's no goal here, and no "right answer." Just savor the experience.

Body Awareness

Place your hand in your lap, palm up. Focus on your hand—examine it in a way you have not done before. What does it feel like? What does it look like? Look inside your hand as well: be aware of its internal structure—how it bends, how it changes when it moves. Hands are miraculous things.

Mindful Listening

Choose a sound—perhaps the sound of the birds in the trees outside. Listen to the sound. Attend to the highs and lows, the rhythm, the repetition, the pauses. Try the same thing near a playground, as you listen to the voices of children. You'll be surprised what you hear when you really listen—how unique it sounds.

Mindful Eating

Pick up a raisin—just one raisin. Note the color, the translucence, and the wrinkled skin. Place it on your tongue, and without biting, roll it around in your mouth. Feel the size and texture and temperature. Let your tongue smooth the skin. Now bite through the skin slowly, and feel the pulp hit your taste buds. Savor the feel, the taste, and the different textures of skin and pulp with tongue and teeth.

If you found these exercises useful and want to try others, a good source for mindfulness exercises is The Guided Meditation Site at www.the-guided-meditation-site.com.

This exercise is more powerful than you'd think—and more challenging. It often takes a number of tries to achieve a full minute of clear, uncluttered attention; some people are never able to do it. But if you can, the payoff will be great. Once you master this exercise, it will be a great tool for moving beyond the worries of the day when distractions threaten to overwhelm you. It can help you move beyond anger during frustrating moments that sometimes occur—those hassles we talked about in chapter 7. (So if you're stuck in bumper-to-bumper traffic and feel your blood pressure starting to go through the roof, try a mindfulness minute and you'll be surprised how much it helps.)

The mindfulness minute is powerful, but there are other exercises you can do as well to learn how to live in the moment and avoid wasting time and energy on pointless things. We list a few of these exercises in the sidebar on page 161.

OPTIMISM: REFRAMING TO DISCOVER THE GOOD

Several decades ago, psychologist Susanne Kobasa studied mid- and senior-level managers in a company that was downsizing due to financial pressures. She wanted to understand how these people—all under considerable duress at the time—coped with the stress and uncertainty. She was hoping to discover what distinguished those employees who thrived in the face of adversity from those who succumbed to depression, anxiety, and illness.

Three factors emerged, and they have emerged time and again in subsequent studies—so much so that they've been given a name: the *hardy personality*. First and foremost, what distinguished those employees who thrived from those who didn't was unflagging optimism—an unshakable belief that, one way or another, things would work out in the end. And as a result they showed three traits—commitment, challenge, and control—that combined to carry them through the uncertainty unscathed:

- **Commitment.** Those employees who fared best shared the belief that once they'd decided on a plan of action they should stay the course and see it through. Call it stubbornness if you want, but commitment helped people feel confident in the path they had chosen, and not waver from that path when obstacles appeared.

- **Challenge.** A core feature of hardiness is the ability to see uncertainty as an expectable feature of life, and challenge as an opportunity for growth and positive change. So to those hardy employees, downsizing didn't mean losing their job; it meant being free to explore other, better options.

- **Control.** Control involves the belief that, no matter how difficult the task or how long the odds, one's efforts will make a difference in determining the outcome. Control helps people take an active approach to challenge rather than adopting a passive wait-and-see attitude. However things turn out, you'll feel better—and fare better—for having made the effort.

As you can see, your attitudes and beliefs have an enormous impact on how you react to life's obstacles. Even though it might not always feel like it, you have more control than you realize over how you perceive yourself and the world.

All Things Must Pass

One of the great challenges of later adulthood is dealing with our awareness (often unspoken) that even the most cherished relationship will eventually end. Some people cope with this by detaching and avoiding loss altogether, but we think that's a bad idea—the costs are too great. It's better to connect with others, enjoy relationships as they grow, and find ways to cope when the inevitable happens.

Psychologists divide the grieving process (sometimes called *grief work*) into three phases; here are some common responses at each stage.

IMMEDIATE REACTIONS TO LOSS

Each of us responds to loss in our own way, and no single response is "better" than another. Expect to experience the following, alone or in combination:

- **Shock.** When faced with the unbearable, mind and body may simply "shut down" for a while. This is nature's way of protecting us—numbing us temporarily so we're not overwhelmed. Shock is normal, and it's usually more frightening to observers than to the person undergoing it (who isn't feeling much of anything).

- **Denial.** No matter how well prepared we are intellectually, we are rarely prepared to deal with death emotionally. Denial has a dreamlike, "this-can't-be-happening" quality to it, and people often report that they feel detached, as if watching events unfold from a distance. Like shock, denial is nature's way of shielding us during a vulnerable time.

- **Breakdown.** Not everyone is blessed with a temporary cocoon of denial. Some people respond to loss with immediate, unrestrained, no-holds-barred grief. Sometimes this period of extreme upset passes by itself, but when breakdown is severe, or lasts longer than a day or two, interventions such as medication or psychotherapy may be needed.

SHORT-TERM COPING

We don't think of these as ways of "coping," but they are: painful though such experiences may be, they help us come to grips with thoughts and feelings triggered by our loss:

- **Depression.** You may feel sad or empty, and be unable to eat, sleep, or concentrate. You might lose interest in your usual activities and withdraw. Some degree of depression is normal, but if depression lingers, contact your physician. (We discussed treatment options for depression in chapter 6.)

- **Anger.** As we think about our loss, we may find ourselves resenting those who are still here—people less giving, "less deserving" of life. The world begins to seem like an unjust place, and sometimes we react in a surprising way: since we can't get angry at the entire world, we take it out on those closest to us (the very people trying hardest to help).

- **Guilt.** The flip side of anger is guilt. (Some psychologists think of guilt as "anger directed inward.") When we finally accept that a loved one is gone, we realize that we've lost our opportunity to correct past mistakes. Guilt often follows, and may deepen as we reflect on things we wish we'd done differently.

>> FUNERAL PLANNING

It might seem morbid (okay, it is), but making your own funeral arrangements has two great benefits. First, you're doing a tremendous service for your family, sparing them the burden of rushed funeral planning in the midst of crisis and loss. It's a gift for those you love.

Second, planning your funeral is a way of reminding yourself that life does not go on forever—that your time here is limited and must be well spent. In that respect, funeral planning is a great mindfulness exercise—it will remind you in no uncertain terms how important it is to make good choices about what you do each day.

Funeral planning is never fun—and it might well stir up some dormant family conflicts (like who gets to bed down next to whom for eternity). But the Internet has made the practical aspects of funeral planning easier than ever. And you can purchase all sorts of funeral gear online. Did you know that one of the main pull-down menu options on Costco's website—right between "Entertainment" and "Furniture and Décor"—is "Funeral"?

Our advice is that you consider purchasing funeral *products* (like urns and caskets) online, but not funeral *services* (there are too many scammers out there ready to take your deposit and disappear). For funeral services, you want to deal with well-established local people who have good reputations in the community. You can obtain information regarding funeral planning (including estimated costs of various products and services) from the National Funeral Directors Association. They can be reached by phone at 800-228-6332; by mail at 13625 Bishop's Drive, Brookfield, WI, 53005; via email at nfda@nfda.org, or on the web at www.nfda.org.

LONG-TERM SURVIVAL

Once you've acknowledged your loss, you can find ways to work through it. Grieving is a long process—months or years, not days or weeks. You can't hurry grief, but you can do things to make the process more meaningful. These include:

- **Finding meaning.** Sometimes we don't realize how important someone was to us until they're gone. Solitary reflection and reminiscing can help with this process; so will intimate talks with friends and those closest to your loved one. These talks allow you to share special memories and free yourself of pent-up sadness, guilt, and pain.

- **Developing personal rituals.** Some people draw comfort from fulfilling formal religious obligations; others find solace in working for causes that were important to that person—making sure that person's life continues to have an impact. Whatever route you choose, make a point of performing some literal, physical acts in honor of your lost loved one. Where grief work is concerned, doing is as important as thinking and feeling.

- **Creating balanced memories.** Right after someone we're close to dies, we tend to focus only on the good: faults are forgotten, hurts forgiven, bad memories denied. This works in the short run, but to grieve effectively, we must face up to the bad as well as the good. No one is perfect, and an important part of grief work involves accepting and acknowledging this. Until we let go of our "sanitized" memories, we can never let go of the grief. But remember: just because someone had flaws, that doesn't mean you didn't love them—or that they didn't love you.

It's taken a long time for the medical community to appreciate the ways that spirituality and optimism help foster healthy living; it's taken even longer for researchers to accept that spirituality is an important aspect of a balanced post-retirement life. It took us a while as well, but in our work with older adults we've come to realize that a healthy spirit is just as important as a healthy mind and healthy body—sometimes more so—and crucial for successful aging in place.

CHAPTER 9

Strengthening Ties with Others

Can you imagine us years from today, sharing a park bench quietly?
How terribly strange to be seventy...
—PAUL SIMON

It's true: when you're young, it's hard to imagine being your parents' age—or your grandparents'. But the years go by, and slowly, subtly, change takes hold; we morph from younger to older adults. Paul Simon wrote those lyrics nearly fifty years ago. He's now in his early 70s.

Just as we change over the years, our relationships change as well. This chapter is about building (or rebuilding) bridges—connecting with others, familiar and new. It's about friendship, family, and late-life romance, and also about love and loss.

Post-Retirement Friendship

For many people, post-retirement social isolation is a major challenge, especially for those who find themselves living alone after having spent many years with a partner. Without the ready-made social circle of work, some of us simply don't know how to connect with others (and sometimes this difficulty was "masked" over the years if one's partner happened to be a social butterfly). It's ironic, but true: many assisted living placements are actually triggered by inadequate social skills and an inability to develop new supportive relationships rather than by actual physical care needs.

It's never too late to sharpen your relationship-building skills—you're always going to need them. Here are a few tips for strengthening existing connections and building new ones:

- **Find things you love, and others will find you.** Join a structured interest group, like a book club or an adult education class, and you're bound to meet people with similar interests. MeetUp.com (www.meetup.com) is a great resource for locating groups in your area—or organizing a group yourself.

- **Share what you know.** If you can embroider, take great (or not so great) photos, or engage in lively political discourse, there's a school, library, or nursing home nearby that would love to have you strut your stuff and share your skills. Check websites and local papers for volunteer opportunities.

>> THE FRIENDSHIP CONTRACT

For friendship to thrive, friends must meet each other's needs. Researchers Michael Argyle and Monica Henderson identified five rules that are part of most people's unspoken "friendship contract":

- Provide emotional support (be a good listener)
- Trust and confide in each other (don't be judgmental—you're not perfect either)
- Give honest feedback and advice (even if it's not what the person wants to hear)
- Pitch in and help in times of need (without having to be asked)
- Be tolerant of each other's friends (including the creepy ones)

- **Adjust your friendship expectations.** Late-life friendships begin more slowly than earlier ones, and often take longer to mature. Your new friends come with considerable baggage (as do you), and likely have a number of competing commitments. You may well play second fiddle to their adult children, grandchildren, and others.

- **Don't count on all your old "couple friends" to stick around.** People who lose a partner through death or divorce are often surprised to discover that they lose many longtime friends as well—some were actually connected to your partner, not you.

- **Be careful not to appear needy or desperate.** Enthusiasm is a lovely thing, but overeager people can be somewhat off-putting. So rather than hovering, take a Zen approach. Be there, and be open and engaging—friendship will come to you.

- **Sometimes companionship is enough.** Not everyone you meet will become your BFF—and that's okay. If your new friend is someone with whom you can dine, or spend an hour or two enjoying the nice weather, that's good too.

Healthy Dependency

Suzanne, a friend of ours, recently told us over dinner that she was concerned regarding her father's increasing reliance on his housekeeper, Magda. We asked why she was worried.

"She picks out all his clothes," Suzanne said. "He never goes shopping without her. And she tells him when he needs to get a haircut! I just think it's odd, don't you?"

We get asked this a lot, and our answer—to Suzanne's obvious disappointment—was, it's actually not all that unusual. Here's the thing: Suzanne's father has limited vision and hearing, and can no longer drive on his own. Suzanne, though devoted to her dad in many ways, isn't willing or able to put her career on hold to take care of his day-to-day needs. And thanks to his housekeeper, Suzanne's father has been able to remain in his home of more than fifty years, aging in place with a bit of extra help. Even his daughter admits he's been eating better (and she's been sleeping better) since Magda arrived.

It's a quirk of American culture—the widespread belief that mature adults must fend for themselves, and go it alone no matter how great the challenge. After all, that's what grown-ups do (or so we're told). But none of us, no matter how strong, can navigate life's waters on our own. *Healthy dependency* is the ability to seek guidance and support from other people appropriately and feel good—not guilty—about asking for help when you need it. Healthy dependency means using the help you receive from others to learn and grow—to confront life's challenges, not shrink from them.

> It's a quirk of American culture—the widespread belief that mature adults must fend for themselves, and go it alone no matter how great the challenge. After all, that's what grown-ups do (or so we're told). But none of us, no matter how strong, can navigate life's waters on our own.

An important caveat here: to understand healthy dependency, you need to look below the surface, beyond behavior, to the underlying goals that shape the behavior. When you adopt this mindset, it becomes easier to see that sometimes we show increased dependency in one area so we can maintain (or even increase) our ability to function autonomously in other areas. Psychologists refer to this as *compensatory dependency* because our enhanced functioning in one domain compensates for our increased dependency in another.

Compensatory dependencies are adaptive (they facilitate successful aging), so don't be too quick to judge. If you show increased dependency in one area of life, analyze the situation to see if this increased dependency may actually be helping you thrive in some other area. If so, it's adaptive—it's healthy dependency. For example, if you're having trouble driving and need help with transportation, but you use this help to join an interest group (like a bridge club) that lets you connect with others, that's okay. If you have a friend who requires in-home care from a visiting nurse or home health aide, and he uses this help to manage his diabetes more effectively so he can continue to live independently, that's healthy—not unhealthy—dependency.

>> HEALTHY DEPENDENCY IN TROUBLING TIMES: BUILDING CONNECTIONS FOR NOW AND LATER

Whether you're a loner or a social butterfly, healthy dependency requires that you make mindful choices so you can get the help you need, strengthen connections, and set the stage for future support. Five strategies are useful:

- **Time your requests.** Don't interrupt someone during their busiest time, but wait until the person is less distracted and less harried. They'll be more receptive to your request and better able to decide without pressure whether they're ready to step up and help.
- **Be flexible.** Not everyone is capable of responding exactly as you'd like, and that's okay. Let people help as they see fit, and be grateful for it—even if it wasn't quite what you were hoping for.
- **Communicate clearly.** It might feel awkward to specify exactly what you want from someone, but it's the best way to avoid misunderstandings and get what you need.
- **Be selective.** Not everyone is comfortable offering help—or receiving it—so be selective when you ask or offer. If you have a friend who's a bit detached, this might not be the best person to turn to when you need to unburden yourself of heavy emotional baggage.
- **'Tis better to give.** Keep in mind that healthy dependency is a two-way street, and it's important that you be sensitive to others' needs as well as your own. Sometimes that means taking the initiative and offering to help without waiting to be asked.

Family Ties

Family members share a great deal—kinship, common history, folklore, culture, attitudes, values, and fears. For many of us, family bonds remain strong throughout life—these are the folks who've "got your back" (and vice versa). Family relationships are particularly complex, but they also present us with a unique opportunity: each day we have the chance to encounter our relatives anew, both as the people we have known forever, and the people they are today. Taking the time to reexamine family ties can help us discover new features in people we've tended to see as one-dimensional and role defined ("my bratty kid brother"). We need not be prisoners of our past—there are many ways of being a family.

CONNECTING (OR RECONNECTING) WITH SIBLINGS

Many people report that they were close to their siblings when they were younger, but drifted apart over time as career and lifestyle choices eroded family bonds—not too surprising given our increasingly mobile society. Others note (usually with considerable puzzlement) that even though they fought all the time as kids, they've now become inseparable, drawn together by some mysterious connection they can't quite put into words. It's ironic, but true: for many sibling pairs, the space that comes from living separate lives actually allows them to reconnect more deeply as adults, moving beyond old patterns and reinventing their relationship.

Beyond the benefits of reconnecting with your long-lost brother or sister, there are two other advantages to reconnecting with siblings post-retirement. First, siblings provide unique (and uniquely valuable) perspective in the face of challenge and loss. For all the comfort and support you may receive from friends following the death of a parent, no one shares your perspective on Mom or Dad as well as your brother or sister does. No one can help you process the memories—the bad as well as the good—as well as those who grew up with you and experienced it all firsthand.

The second reason to reconnect is more practical: siblings often become the primary caregiver for a brother or sister whose health has begun to decline. This is especially true if the person in declining health is without a partner, but even for people who are still part of a couple, in many cases it's the sibling—not the partner—who manages many of the everyday tasks (like shopping and bill paying) that are crucial for aging in place. Sometimes two siblings may even become mutual caregivers if they experience different challenges (for example, you might help with transportation if your sister's eyesight is failing, and she in return can be your "orienting cue" if memory begins to fade).

>> WHAT IF YOU DON'T GET ALONG?

On his deathbed, a man handed his wife a letter, and asked her to read it aloud at his funeral. She opened the letter after he died. It was a lengthy, bitter castigation of their youngest son, with whom her husband had always had a conflicted relationship. After some brief but intense soul-searching, she burned the letter and never told her family that it existed. In this way, she felt she'd preserved her husband's dignity and protected her son's feelings.

Many years later this woman told us that she was at peace with the choice she'd made, but since she was sharing this in the context of thera-peutic life review shortly before her own death, one thing is certain: even years after the event it still lingered in her mind as a key moment—a key choice point—in her life.

It comforts some to think that despite all the battles, in the end fam-ily members really do appreciate how much they love each other. Well, not always. In fact, there are a lot of people who genuinely dislike their parents (or their children or siblings)—and sometimes with good rea-son. The father who burdened you with the knowledge that you were an unwanted child, the brother who ridiculed you mercilessly in front of everyone at school, the daughter who spurned your deeply held faith traditions—all represent complex betrayals that affect our relationships in fundamental ways.

There's no ideal solution to such sticky situations. Some people choose to sever these relationships altogether, preventing further con-flict, but also losing the opportunity to reconnect and learn something about forgiveness, acceptance, and tolerance. Other people spend a life-time working ceaselessly to repair these fractured family ties, trying in vain to find some way of making them work however painful they may be.

And sometimes two family members simply coexist, with minimal contact, neither accepting nor rejecting each other, but avoiding each other judiciously through decades of family gatherings. (The persis-tence of these patterns can be truly remarkable: one of us had two aunts who—so the story goes—fought over a boyfriend in high school. Fifty years later they still refused to acknowledge each other's existence.)

THE "SORT OF" FAMILY: RELATIVES BY MARRIAGE

Although most everyone has at least one good story about outrageous in-law behavior—holidays and weddings are endless sources of amusement—there's been surprisingly little research on family-by-marriage relationships. Too bad, because your partner's family often assumes a central role in your social network once you tie the knot.

It's safe to say that many romantic partnerships connect groups of people who would otherwise never have met—or tolerated each other if they had. How else would bookish introverts wind up spending Thanksgiving with beer-stoked football fans, or cutting-edge fashion designers with tradition-minded homebodies? While you might not look forward to these slightly surreal interactions, if you learn to see them as an escape from the ordinary (or a field trip to the strange), they can actually become memorable, consciousness-raising experiences. (Just file them under "Travel and Exploration," discussed in chapter 8.)

Of course, things don't always work out well when "oil and water" families interact. We learned this the hard way when we tried to introduce our two sets of parents after we announced our engagement. For some reason, our families couldn't connect: their backgrounds were just too different, their values too dissimilar. After a few aborted efforts on the part of Bob's parents, both sides decided they'd coexist in separate worlds. And that's the way things stayed: our two sets of parents never met, never corresponded, never spoke on the phone. A lost opportunity is how we see it.

HEALING RIFTS WITH YOUR ADULT CHILDREN

It's more common than we think: surveys indicate 20 percent of retirees—one in five—report that they have difficult or conflicted relationships with their adult children (some surveys actually put this number at 30 percent). There's even a website available to discuss these rifts, unburden yourself, and connect with others in similar circumstances (www.estrangedstories.com).

Healing longstanding rifts with adult children can be a challenge (and sometimes it's just not possible—the wounds are too deep). But if this is an issue for you or your partner, here are a few tips:

- **Take responsibility for your mistakes, even if they were well-intentioned.** Doing this may mean swallowing your pride, but if it opens up the lines of communication, it's worth it in the long run.

- **Try to see things through your child's eyes.** Even if you disagree, it's helpful to understand your son's or daughter's perspective (and whatever you do, resist the urge to guilt trip—reminding your child how hurtful their absence has been will never help).

- **Be patient.** Sometimes it takes multiple attempts before a longstanding rift can be healed, so don't expect success on the first attempt. (Hope for it, but don't expect it.)

- **Be flexible.** When hurt runs deep, healing may be incomplete, so even if things don't end up exactly as you'd hoped, if the situation improves somewhat that might be enough.

- **Don't draw others into the dialogue.** Even if you mean well, reaching out to your child through a partner or friend may be interpreted by them as yet another violation of trust.

Love across the Years

Dating after 50 brings its own unique challenges. Meeting people in bars and nightclubs frequented by a younger crowd no longer seems like such a good idea (seriously, don't—no matter how fabulous your hairpiece). Since some of the old familiar options are gone, you'll need to be a bit more creative here. There are websites tailored to retirement-age adults who want to connect with others (we'll discuss these in a moment). And the traditional face-to-face strategy is still an option, even if the venue has changed. Consider these possibilities:

- **Clubs and interest groups.** The beauty of this approach is that you'll be sure to encounter people whose interests overlap with yours; conversation comes more naturally.

- **Adult education classes.** Ditto for adult education courses: you're all there because you find the topic interesting. An added plus: you'll have opportunities to chat while you wait for class to begin—and opportunities for post-class socializing at a nearby diner, restaurant, or bar, either with one person or a larger group.

- **Volunteer activities.** The challenge here is that you might actually be too busy working to sit down and chat. On the other hand, it's clear that everyone feels passionate about the same things, so you have a ready-made connection to draw upon (plus the bonding that comes from a shared volunteer experience helps ease the transition to friendship—or more).

- **Senior centers.** This is not everyone's idea of a place to meet potential dates, but then again, you never know.

>> ALONE OR WITH OTHERS? A FUNDAMENTAL CHOICE

Connecting with others can take many different forms, and it works best if you do it in a way that fits your style. If you're single, widowed, or divorced, an important lifestyle choice is in order: do you prefer to live alone or with other people?

Two principles—history and habits, personality and preferences—can help guide your thinking in this area:

Consider Your History and Habits

If you hail from a big family and grew up in a house that was always full of visitors, the thought of living alone may seem quite horrifying. If you grew up alone, an only child, the idea of sharing your kitchen or bathroom with another person might feel strange. Circumstances sometimes require that you endure a less-than-ideal mix for a while, but settling on a permanent living situation that conflicts with a lifetime of experience rarely works well.

If you can tolerate others in your space, consider it. Numerous studies have found that people with many social ties tend to age happily and gracefully. Developing an accepting attitude is important here, and it

ONLINE DATING

You'd be surprised how many online dating sites aimed at the 50+ crowd are out there—until you realize how many people in this age group are back on the dating scene. Even the mainstream companies (like eHarmony and match.com) have separate areas of their websites for over-50 matchmaking.

A few ground rules:

- **Creating an effective profile.** One of the quirks of the Internet is that people get bored more quickly than if they're reading text on a page, so you need to get right to the point. Wow them with your opening sentence—it has to be a real grabber. Then tell your story—the story of who you are—but not in too much detail (check out existing profiles to get a sense of what others are doing).

helps if you can be tolerant of others' oddities and quirks. (You have them too, even if you don't see them.)

Know Your Personality and Preferences

Habits are important, but temperament matters too: research suggests that longstanding personality traits—everything from optimism and openness to suspiciousness and mistrust—tend to become more pronounced as we age. People who grew up shy often become veritable hermits later in life. Fighting these trends is rarely successful (they're rooted in our basic biology), so it's wise to "go with the flow" and choose a lifestyle that accommodates your personality.

If you need solitude to be happy but find yourself sharing space with others, try to reserve some private time, and let those around you know about your privacy needs. If you hate being by yourself and your solo apartment seems to echo with emptiness, see if there's a senior center nearby where you can find people to interact with on a regular basis. To connect with people here (and elsewhere), try to develop some common ground of mutual interest—card playing, for example—that allows you to interact comfortably even with those you've just met.

Edit your profile carefully before posting it to be sure it says exactly what you want, and has the right "feel" to it as well (not too heavy, not too light). And do be sure to edit for grammar and punctuation; nothing ensures online failure like a profile full of typos.

- **Starting the conversation.** Don't rush into a face-to-face meeting—it's better to begin by phone or an email exchange. If you do go either of these routes, don't feel pressured to move ahead too quickly—two or three predate phone chats is normal. (If you're feeling rushed by a prospective date to move things forward more quickly than you'd like, that's a big red flag.) Expect a few glitches (awkward moments, miscommunications) on both sides; you're both nervous, so a bit of interpersonal clumsiness is normal. And even if things go better than expected, try not be become infatuated and convinced that you've stumbled upon Mr. (or Ms.) right. Puppy love isn't limited to 20-year-olds; you might be experiencing it again, 40 or 50 years later. Good for you—enjoy it! But take your time. . .

- **The first date.** It's usually best to meet in a public place (like a bar or restaurant) rather than getting together at home. A public meeting takes some of the pressure off—and you can make a quick exit if things really go south. Meeting for a drink or dinner is most traditional, but if you're nervous and want things to proceed more slowly, suggest lunch instead. As always, appearance matters: if you've been away from the dating scene for a while, you might not be familiar with today's norms, so don't overdress or underdress (if you're unsure, business casual is always a good choice). And choose "safe" topics for conversation. No potential paramour wants to hear about your health problems, your messy divorce, or your saintly ex-partner who can never be replaced. Whatever you do, avoid politics and religion—both are conversation minefields. Instead stick to neutral topics like hobbies, interests, travel plans (or past travel experiences), and things like favorite foods (a good test of how flexible and adventuresome your date might be).

- **Staying safe.** It's always better to take extra precautions, even if you feel a bit silly doing so. Tell someone (a friend or relative) where you're going, and with whom, and let your date know that you did this, but subtly. (You can always make light of it by blaming your "overprotective friend.") Don't give away too much personal information on a first date—there's time for that later. And by all means, drink in moderation. You don't want to make a bad impression by drinking too much (or worse, put yourself in an unsafe situation).

LONG-DISTANCE ROMANCE

It's more common than you'd think: the US Census Bureau estimates that more than a million married couples age 50+ live apart for reasons other than separation or marital strife. Oftentimes these long-distance romances result from job considerations; sometimes they stem from family responsibilities, as when one partner relocates temporarily to care for an aging parent.

Long-distance relationships are also fairly common among couples who reconnect after years (sometimes decades) of being apart. Sometimes adolescent and young adult romances that fizzled in response to family disapproval or circumstances beyond the young folks' control actually blossom decades later when those issues no longer exist. These sorts of "late-life reconnections" have always occurred—now with the benefit of social networking sites like Facebook, it's easier than ever to find out where your old flame ended up after all these years.

Whatever the reason, if you're part of a couple who's "living apart together" (that's what they call it these days), several strategies can help ease the burden:

- **Cyberconnect.** Frequent phone chats are definitely in order; Skype (or a similar online communication service) can provide additional face-to-face contact.

- **Vary the length of visits.** It's tempting to maximize the number of visits even if that means keeping them short, but it's helpful to include the occasional longer trip as well (think five to seven days rather than the usual one or two). If you limit yourself to weekend get-togethers, you'll feel as though you're always moving straight from unpacking to getting ready to leave.

- **Use together time wisely.** Prioritizing is important here. Solitary activities (like jogging) should take a backseat to things you do together.

- **Set an end date.** Living apart is stressful, and it's important that you have an end date in mind. Even if you're not certain when you'll be able to live together again, set an actual date—and change it if need be.

> ## >> LATE-LIFE ROMANCE: GENDER MATTERS
>
> Whether this seems fair and just will probably depend on your gender, but facts are facts, and there's little we can do to change them. Where late-life romance is concerned, it pays to be male. Consider:
>
> - Because women live longer, the gender balance shifts in later adulthood. Although earlier in life, things are pretty even, the ratio of women to men age 60+ is 100 to 83.
>
> - In part because of this gender shift, 80 percent of men over age 60 are still married versus 48 percent of women aged 60+.
>
> - A higher proportion of older women than older men live alone post-retirement (19 percent of women versus 9 percent of men).
>
> - For every 100 women over 60 living without a partner, there are only 33 partner-less men.

Twenty-First Century Networking: The New Media

Email has been around long enough that it no longer qualifies as new. Ditto for texting (also called "instant messaging"), basically a way of sending an "instant email" (usually brief) to one or more people. You've probably seen the pared-down language of texting, which takes the form of phrases like *cn u blv it . . . lol!* (Can you believe it . . . laugh out loud!)

Now there's *new* new media—and it's evolving so quickly our description will likely be outdated by the time you're reading this. (But that's why we created aging-wisely.com—we'll keep you updated.) For now, here are

three media platforms you should know about—they'll be handy for networking with family, friends, and others:

- **Facebook.** The granddaddy of social media sites, Facebook now has
  more than one billion users (and counting). It's become the homepage
  of a generation, though more and more adults in their 50s and beyond
  are signing up. In some ways, Facebook is the most permanent form of
  popular social media; many users' Facebook pages are elaborate con-
  structions involving hundreds—even thousands—of photos, updates,
  and other personal artifacts, and unless they're deliberately removed,
  they'll remain in cyberspace forever. (Well, as long as Facebook
  exists, anyway.) Facebook is great for reconnecting with childhood,
  high school, and college friends (especially useful if you relocated to
  retire). Many people who move to a new area post-retirement report
  that Facebook connections are very helpful during the transition
  period, enabling them to feel connected with others as they gradually
  develop a new circle of friends.

- **Twitter.** Deliberately designed for rapid, informal communication,
  Twitter messages are limited to 140 characters max. Some users
  embed web links in Twitter messages (which allows you to send along
  larger amounts of information via the link), and many people "tweet"
  multiple times each day. Twitter has become a required form of communication for celebrities, and celebrity wannabes as well; it's also
  used by authors and bloggers to spread the word regarding their work.
  One advantage of Twitter is that as you tweet, you'll gain "followers"—
  people who sign on to follow your tweets because they like what you
  have to say. The reverse is true, too, of course, and in addition to following individuals, you can also follow organizations (like AARP) so
  you receive up-to-the-minute info on aging-related topics.

- **Tumblr.** This is a site for blogging, reblogging (passing along existing
  blogs to others), and microblogging (posting very brief blogs to get
  your message out quickly); Tumblr users also create photosets (collec-
  tions of photos linked by a common theme), stream video, and post
  text. Tumblr's platform has some unique features (like the capacity

for users to blog collaboratively, even from a distance, with different contributors adding, revising, and so on), and the site has grown from one million blogs in 2009 to more than forty million today. Tumblr is best suited to those who have interests and ideas that they want to share with others through blogs. A hidden advantage of the Tumblr platform, which emphasizes shared blogs and "reblogging" (passing along existing blogs to others), is that by collaborating you connect with people who share your interests, attitudes, and ideals.

In addition to these well-established platforms there are a number of social networking sites aimed specifically at people age 50+. MyBoomerPlace, GenKvetch, and AARP's online community are among the best; we provide contact info for these in the Resource and Contact Information section at the back of the book.

This might well be the first (and only) time you'll see senior centers discussed alongside blogging and online dating, but hopefully their common features (and value) are now clear: it doesn't matter *how* you connect, but *that* you connect. Building bridges—rediscovering old ties and creating new ones—is an essential component of a happy, healthy retirement.

CHAPTER 10

Giving Back

On June 27, 2008, Microsoft cofounder Bill Gates ended his active involvement in the company so he could devote more of his time to philanthropy through the Bill and Melinda Gates Foundation. The foundation has donated more than $30 billion to various charitable causes, and Bill and Melinda Gates have deliberately taken a "hands-on" approach, visiting impoverished regions of the world to see firsthand the impact of their foundation's grants. Inspired in part by the Gates Foundation's initial success, Warren Buffett donated an additional $30 billion to the cause. In 2010 Bill Gates, Warren Buffett, and Mark Zuckerberg signed the "Gates-Buffett Giving Pledge," each promising to donate more than half of their assets to charity during the coming years.

Few of us are as well off as Mark Zuckerberg, Bill Gates, or Warren Buffett, but any of us, no matter how modest our lifestyle or income, can make a difference. Consider, for example, Robert Young of Bellevue, Washington, who sold his successful outdoor clothing business and moved to Bozeman, Montana, where he started the nonprofit Red Feather Development Group, which builds low-cost homes for Native Americans living below the poverty line. Or Dale Dunning of Lewes, Delaware, who wakes up every day at 2 a.m. to prepare meals for those who can't afford to feed themselves; Dale estimates that she and her husband, Ken, a state utilities worker, spend about $7,000 of their own money each year purchasing ingredients. Dale's explanation for her generosity is simple: "I want people to know that someone cares."

This final chapter is about creating and shaping your legacy—it's about making a lasting impact by giving back. We discuss various options for monetary donations, of course, but we also discuss "hands-on" ways of giving like sharing your wisdom and expertise.

Mindful Gifting: The Buck Starts Here

In these sections, we focus on financial contributions, and two issues are central: choosing where (and how) you'd like to invest your funds, and doing it in such a way that you get maximum "bang for your buck."

WHERE THE HEART IS

Donating your hard-earned savings to others works best when you do it in ways you find meaningful, supporting those causes in which you truly believe. Four strategies to help guide your thinking:

- **Find your passion, then fund it.** Don't rush to contribute to an organization just to "do something" (or worse, because you've been pressured to contribute by a representative of that organization). Take the time to discover which causes you believe in most strongly—those you can feel good about supporting for the long term.

- **If your means are modest, keep it local.** National and international charities can have a tremendous impact (think UNICEF or the International Red Cross), but if your means are modest, you might want to consider supporting some local causes in addition to, or in lieu of, larger organizations. A few thousand (or even a few hundred) dollars can make a world of difference at your local food bank.

- **Consider your range of options.** Don't limit your contribution to charitable organizations with which you're already familiar—there might be others out there that are closer to your heart. Medical research foundations, social service organizations, schools, religious institutions, museums, symphonies, cultural centers, advocacy groups—all are worth considering. And once you've narrowed your range of possibilities, do that last bit of legwork to be sure it's an organization that keeps overhead costs low so your money is used efficiently. (More on that in a bit.)

> National and international charities can have a tremendous impact, but if your means are modest, you might want to consider supporting some local causes. A few thousand (or even a few hundred) dollars can make a world of difference at your local food bank.

- **Nonprofits, family, and friends.** Many people combine charitable giving with gifts to relatives and friends. This can also be a great way to maximize impact (for example, by helping fund your grandchild's education). One advantage of this type of gifting is that you can experience the impact firsthand—you'll actually see how your money made a difference.

>> CHOOSING A NONPROFIT

Although there is no single legal definition of a nonprofit organization, in general nonprofit organizations are those created specifically to achieve a purpose other than generating and accumulating money. A nonprofit organization is not precluded from engaging in profit-making activities, but it is prohibited from passing along these profits to founders, directors, officers, or employees. (However, the nonprofit may still pay reasonable salaries to officers, employees, and others who perform a service for it.)

As you might expect, nonprofits differ substantially with respect to how closely they follow these guidelines, how efficiently they use your funds, and other salient features: some nonprofits are better than others. You can get current information on various nonprofits, along with ratings of key efficiency factors, on several websites, including www .charitynavigator.org, www.charitywatch.org, and greatnonprofits.org. In addition, we've provided a checklist you can use to evaluate and compare nonprofits on page 222.

>> DONATING PROPERTY

You'll want to be conservative when determining the value of donated property—many people overestimate how much their stuff is worth. (Just because you're attached to your old cashmere sweater doesn't mean it's a hot item.) Keep in mind that unrealistic valuations of donated property can trigger an IRS audit, which is not worth the extra fifty bucks you made by estimating that your battered 1970s-era TV stand is worth $250.

The IRS website (www.irs.gov) provides guidelines for determining the fair market value of donated property. In addition, here are a few tips:

- In general, you cannot take a deduction for clothing or household items you donate unless the clothing or items are in "good used condition." If you donate clothing or a household item that is not in good used condition, you must include a qualified appraisal of it with your tax return.

- The fair market value of used clothing and other personal items is usually far less than the price you paid for them. Unfortunately, there are no fixed formulas or methods for finding the value of used items of clothing; you should try to value each item at the price buyers of similar items typically pay in used-clothing stores, such as consignment or thrift shops.

- If you contribute property with a fair market value that is more than your original cost basis (for example, a work of art that is now worth more than you paid for it), things get complicated quickly. Consult a tax planner on this.

- When you donate one or more large-ticket items (cars, boats, or airplanes), be especially careful to obtain a valid estimate by a qualified professional—the IRS is likely to scrutinize such donations carefully.

- For any noncash donation exceeding $5,000 in value, you must file additional paperwork (currently IRS Form 8282).

- You can't get a tax deduction for donating food (for example, to a local food bank or homeless shelter). As far as the IRS is concerned, food isn't property.

THE TAXMAN COMETH

Once you've decided where you'd like your money to go, a practical challenge emerges—fending off Uncle Sam. Charitable giving to nonprofits is easy: all the funds go directly to the organization (no tax bite), and you may even get a personal tax deduction as well (consult with your financial planner on this). Where gifting to family and friends is concerned, you should know the pros and cons of different modes of disbursement, so you can choose those that enable you to manage taxes effectively. Four strategies are particularly common, and you'll want to be familiar with each:

- **Gifts.** According to 2012 IRS guidelines, a person may give an unlimited number of recipients cash gifts of up to $13,000 per year, and the recipients don't owe a penny in tax. If a person receives a gift of $13,000 each year from you for ten (or even fifty) years, that person still owes no tax whatsoever on the gifts—they are not counted as income. Two people can give $13,000 each to the same individual, so it's possible for a couple to give a total of $52,000 each year to their child and his or her partner ($13,000 each to the child and $13,000 each to the partner) without triggering any sort of tax event. There's currently a $5 million lifetime limit on these annual gifts (they're called "present interest gifts" in the IRS guidelines; check www.irs.gov for details).

- **Trusts**. A trust is a legal entity used to hold money, property, and other assets. Trusts come in many forms, and most are quite complicated. At this point, you'll likely be dealing with a "living trust" ("testamentary trusts" are established after a person dies). But even here, you must choose between a *revocable living trust* and an *irrevocable living trust*. The best advice we can give you is to consult with experts before you make a move in this arena. It is virtually impossible to set up a trust properly without the advice of an attorney and financial planner. You'll have to pay some consulting fees, but it's worth it— you'll save money in the long run, and avoid making a potentially catastrophic (and irreversible) financial decision.

- **Qualified tuition programs ("529 plans").** A relative newcomer to the gifting scene, 529 plans are educational savings plans operated by a state or educational institution. (Every state in the United States now has at least one 529 plan, and most colleges and universities do as well.) The 529 plans come in two basic forms: *savings plans* (which are similar to a 401(k) or IRA), and *prepaid plans* (which let you prepay the costs of tuition and other higher education expenses, like books and lab supplies, "locking in" today's fees even if the recipient won't be attending school for some time). You can allocate the funds to any qualified beneficiary, divide them among two or more beneficiaries, or shift funds from one beneficiary to another. However, financial details differ from state to state and plan to plan, so it's best to consult with a financial planner before you invest.

>> WHO MAY QUALIFY AS A BENEFICIARY IN YOUR 529 PLAN?

The list is broader than you might think. According to current IRS guidelines, qualified members of the beneficiary's family include the following (and within IRS limits you can allocate the funds however you like):

- Your spouse
- Son, daughter, stepchild, foster child, adopted child, or a descendant of any of them
- Brother, sister, stepbrother, or stepsister
- Father or mother, or ancestor of either
- Stepfather or stepmother
- Son or daughter of a brother or sister
- Brother or sister of your father or mother
- Son-in-law, daughter-in-law, father-in-law, mother-in-law, brother-in-law, or sister-in-law
- The spouse of any individual listed above
- First cousin or second cousin

>> HOW *NOT* TO STRUCTURE YOUR WILL

Your will is first and foremost a legal document—a set of instructions regarding the disposition of your assets—but keep in mind that it's also a document with a great deal of emotional baggage for your relatives and others close to you. People have expectations (almost always unstated) regarding what might be left to them, and make no mistake: correct or not, people will draw strong conclusions regarding how you "really" felt about them based on how they're treated in your will.

We obviously can't tell you how to divide up your assets—that's a purely personal decision—but we do have some advice regarding how *not* to structure this document. Two errors are particularly problematic:

- **Including unrealistic restrictions.** We knew a woman who put a caveat in her will stating that if either of her sons placed her in a nursing home, that son would be completely disinherited. We understand the woman's fears, of course, but think about the difficult situation she created. Sometimes people need skilled nursing care, and although no one welcomes this possibility, in certain situations it's simply the best option. Should that situation ever arise, this woman's sons must now choose between getting their mother the most appropriate care and retaining their share of the inheritance.

- **Spreading decision-making authority among multiple people.** Certain assets (like houses) can't be divided. In such situations, it's sometimes tempting to leave the asset to a group of people (for example, one's siblings or one's children), and that's okay. But if you do take that route, be sure to delegate decision-making authority to one person rather than the entire group. We know a couple who took the latter route, and now, after more than a decade, the house sits empty, in disrepair, because the owners—three siblings—can't agree on whether they should sell it, rent it, or allow one of the siblings to occupy it. (Not only is the house decaying as the process drags on, but the siblings' relationships have been permanently damaged by years' worth of arguments and legal battles.)

- **Wills.** The Last Will and Testament (usually referred to simply as a *will*) is a document that formalizes a person's wishes concerning the disposition of property, guardianship of minor children, and administration of the estate after his or her death. A will can help preserve assets for one's heirs by minimizing fees and taxes. However, a will does not enable one to avoid *probate*, the court-supervised proceedings that formally conclude a person's legal and financial matters after death. In fact, a will is essentially a written set of instructions for the probate court (hence, it can speed the process considerably). As you plan and draft your will, you'll need to name your *executor*—the person or organization (it could be a bank) responsible for handling the will and managing the probate process. (One other note: We're not fans of Internet will-creation services. Many are legitimate businesses—though some are not—but your will is an important asset management tool, and even a small error or omission can create huge problems down the line. True, consulting with an attorney to draft a will can cost several hundred dollars or more if your estate is complicated, but it's worth it to be sure that things are done correctly.)

Pay It Forward: Hands-On Giving

Financial contributions are not the only way to give back—or give forward. Many people prefer hands-on giving in lieu of (or in addition to) financial support. The possibilities are endless; here are four good ones—teaching, mentoring, volunteering, and civic engagement. Let's take a look at each.

TEACHING: SHARING YOUR WISDOM

There is a range of options here depending upon how much time you want to devote to the effort. Many community colleges, colleges, and universities hire people with professional expertise and experience to teach undergraduate or graduate courses. If you go this route, you'll likely be hired as an adjunct faculty member, listed on the department website, and be paid a preset amount ($3,000 to $5,000 per course is about average these days) to teach a semester-long class (figure fifteen weeks). If you'd prefer to make a more modest time commitment, many school districts and community colleges sponsor adult education courses (often with titles like Investing Made Easy, Gardening for Dummies, and Internet Basics) that are taught by local professionals. Most of these classes meet for one or two evenings, and though they pay virtually nothing, it can be a fun experience—and a great way to connect with people in the community.

MENTORING: THE BENEFIT OF EXPERIENCE

Here, too, several options present themselves. Many retirees mentor younger people who aspire to enter their field; if you do this, you'll be passing along your wisdom and experience to the next generation of professionals. But mentoring need not be limited to professional issues—you can also pass on more personal life skills. If you've raised your own children, you might want to mentor new, inexperienced parents. If you feel a strong commitment to your faith traditions, you can help guide those new to the faith (or those struggling with doubts). You might also consider leading a group for younger members of your church, synagogue, or mosque.

Another option is to mentor members of an underserved group—people in need of some extra guidance and support (Big Brothers/Big Sisters is one of the more familiar names in this area). If you are a lesbian, gay, bisexual or transgendered person and feel centered and confident in your sexual orientation, you can provide some much-needed support to those struggling with these issues; the National Coalition for LGBT Health (www.lgbthealth.webolutionary.com) offers great information for getting involved.

An additional possibility—though this is not for everyone involves mentoring based on some sort of unusual personal experience. If you've battled a serious illness, for example, lived through the loss of a child or a partner, or recovered from an addiction, those who are now navigating these challenges would benefit tremendously from your insights. And if you're truly ambitious and would like to start your own mentoring organization, the Mentoring Center (www.mentor.org) provides advice, information, and resources.

VOLUNTEER WORK: ON THE FRONT LINES

Some volunteer opportunities draw upon your professional expertise (as when retired accountants help people with modest means file their income taxes at no cost). Others let you share well-honed life skills like reading—you can become involved in literacy programs for immigrants and adults who lacked the benefit of formal education through your local library. If you're multilingual, you may be able to provide translation services for hospitals and social service agencies, or teach English as a Second Language (ESL) at a local college or community center. (Note that teaching ESL may require training and certification, depending upon the setting in which you plan to work; you can learn more through the TESOL International Association website at www.tesol.org.)

Volunteering at a nearby hospital or food bank is another possibility; Meals on Wheels is always looking for people to prepare and deliver meals for housebound older adults. (Check out their website at www.mowaa.org.) The Veterans Administration provides a variety of services and supports for military families through their Wounded Warrior initiative. Some correctional institutions offer innovative programs to lend support to the families of incarcerated prisoners (facilitating visits, providing transportation for partners and children, and so on).

For the more adventurous among us, volunteering in an impoverished region of the United States is a possibility (Appalachia, for example), as is volunteering overseas (we have a friend who just returned from two years in Benin, on Africa's west coast, where he helped set up a system to provide clean drinking water in rural villages). Habitat for Humanity International (www.habitat.org) and other, similar programs are almost always looking for those with these sorts of practical skills (and those who are willing to learn). Ditto for the International Red Cross—usually among the first to arrive when a catastrophe occurs.

Don't see what you're looking for in any of the above? The Corporation for National & Community Service (www.serve.gov) can link you to a wide array of volunteer options; it will also connect you with Senior Corps, which offers a variety of service opportunities including the Foster Grandparent program and the Senior Companion program, where seniors help seniors who need some assistance with ADLs. A nonprofit group called VolunteerMatch specializes in connecting aspiring volunteers with organizations looking for people with their skill set (www.volunteermatch.org). You might also get some ideas from Action Without Borders (www.idealist.org), and Volunteers of America (www.voa.org). It's worth exploring any or all of these sites—you'll likely find that a lot of organizations are eager to put your energy, enthusiasm, and talents to work.

CIVIC ENGAGEMENT: SHAPING SOCIETY

Though strictly speaking it's not really charitable work, civic engagement offers myriad opportunities to donate your time and energy to a cause in which you believe. Possibilities range from supporting a local or national candidate for public office, to running for office yourself (in many smaller communities, town supervisors, board members, and even mayoral candidates are often community members—political novices rather than career politicians). If there's a social movement about which you feel strongly (reducing domestic violence or impaired driving, perhaps, or changing immigration laws and policies), becoming involved can be very rewarding indeed.

Immortality: A Personal Legacy

Everyone wants to be remembered fondly, and studies indicate that one of our greatest fears as we move from middle to later adulthood (and especially after we retire) is that we'll be forgotten when we're gone. Many people (especially those who intend to give a sizable sum to a single organization) opt for a "named gift"—a gift that will carry your name forward through the years. What better way to create a legacy of personal impact?

There are many venues through which you can give a gift that represents you and carries your legacy forward through the years. Here are three:

- **Gifts in your name or your family name.** Some people want their legacy to be something solid, something concrete (literally). If it's important to you that your legacy be commemorated on a plaque—or some similar marker—you have many options. You can fund anything from a seat in a theater (usually available for a few hundred dollars) to a gallery in a museum (now we're talking about a more substantial sum). One can make even larger gifts or bequests (bequests are gifts given after death, usually via a will or trust), of course—for example, helping fund a campus building. And how about this: in 1992, Henry and Betty Rowan donated $100 million to Glassboro State College in New Jersey; on March 21, 1997, it was officially renamed Rowan University.

- **Funding an activity.** This can take many forms, from funding a scholarship or research award to creating an endowment whose

You might not think this strategy would work, but it does: studies show that once we turn down a large request, we are actually more likely to agree to a smaller request (perhaps out of guilt, or because the smaller request seems cheap by comparison).

- **The reciprocity strategy.** Charitable organizations use this all the time: they cause you to feel indebted by treating you to a fancy dinner, or something along those lines. You are then more likely to agree to their requests because you feel that you owe them something in return for the nice treatment you received. Anytime you receive a gift from a representative of a charitable organization and are then asked to donate, the reciprocity strategy is at work.

- **The group pressure approach.** Most of us underestimate how difficult it is to resist group pressure, even if the "pressure" is never stated directly. If a representative of an organization brings together a group of potential donors, makes a pitch, and then asks for contributions, don't be surprised if you feel intense pressure to contribute along with the others, and in comparable amounts. After all, if you don't, you'll look like you're being cheap (and don't think the organization isn't counting on that—it's a powerful motivating tool). Some unscrupulous organizations even plant confederates in the group who offer large—but imaginary—donations so others will follow suit.

profits are used to support student travel. You can use funds to support volunteer work in a hospital, nursing home, rehabilitation center, or hospice organization. One great advantage of funding an activity is that you'll have the opportunity to experience firsthand the impact of your donation, and if it's invested wisely, it will continue helping others indefinitely.

- **Organ or cell donation.** As we see it, there are two basic strategies for assuring that your body lives on after you're gone. You can take the Walt Disney approach and have your severed head frozen in the hope that someday they'll figure out how to revive your sleeping brain, or you can donate organs (or cells) so that they may be used to help other people survive and thrive. We recommend the latter strategy; the sidebar below outlines the basics of organ donation. (Turns out, by the way, that Walt Disney never really had his body frozen—that's an urban legend. Walt Disney was actually cremated on December 17, 1966, and his ashes are interred at Forest Lawn Memorial Park in Glendale, CA.)

>> ORGAN DONATION: MOVING BEYOND STEREOTYPES

Anyone who saw Monty Python's *The Meaning of Life* will never forget the scene: a man signed up to donate his organs but apparently failed to read the fine print—now the medics were at his door, instruments in hand, ready to harvest.

The medical community must hate that scene—it propagates every stereotype imaginable regarding organ donation, and then some. Given that more than one hundred thousand people are currently awaiting donated organs in the United States alone (equivalent to the entire population of Berkeley, CA), anything that stokes people's fears and trepidations is unhelpful, to say the least. For accurate, up-to-date information—including practical information regarding how to sign up—visit the Department of Health and Human Service's website, www.organdonor.gov.

Organ donation might not be for everyone, but you should make your decision mindfully, not based on misperception and stereotype. Here are myths, and then the facts:

MYTH: If I sign a donor card, hospital staff won't work as hard to save me.

FACT: Physicians and nurses do not "throw in the towel" more quickly on organ donors in the hopes of obtaining spare parts. (In

If you've ever been a writer you'll understand: sometimes when you finish hitting the keys you're surprised where you ended up. Sure, we had a plan for how this book would end—and lots of helpful feedback from our editors, colleagues, and friends. Did we think that the last chapter in *How to Age in Place* would finish with a joke about Walt Disney's frozen head? No we did not. But why not? As George Burns observed (at age 100, no less), the secret to a long life is being able to laugh at yourself.

fact, people who have agreed to organ donation are actually tested more extensively than nondonors before being declared dead.)

MYTH: If I'm in my 60s, I'm too old to donate.
FACT: You can't be too old to donate—there is no age limit on organ donation. Organs have been transplanted successfully many times from donors in their 70s and 80s.

MYTH: If I donate my organs, I can't have an open-casket funeral.
FACT: Completely untrue—no matter what you donate (organs, bone, retinas, even skin), all evidence of the procedure will be hidden, and an open-casket funeral is fine.

MYTH: It will cost my family money.
FACT: Nope—the donor's family is never charged for donating. (Those costs are borne by the recipient.)

MYTH: It's against my religion.
FACT: Most branches of Catholicism, Protestantism, Islam, and Judaism permit organ donation, and if you're at all unsure, you can speak with your local clergy. Or check www.organdonor.gov, which provides guidelines regarding organ donation for different religious denominations.

Looking Forward

Two roads diverged in a wood, and I—
I took the one less traveled by,
And that has made all the difference.
—ROBERT FROST

People often speak of retirement as a time to relax and reflect—to look back on your accomplishments and savor the fruits of your labors. We agree—to a point. One important theme that we hope shined through every chapter in *How to Age in Place* is that retirement is not just a time to look back and reminisce, but it's also an opportunity to look forward, set new goals, and make choices about the person you want to become.

Take a moment, and imagine what you'd like your life to be ten years from now. Are you traveling? Settled down? Spending time with grandchildren? Doing charitable work? In a new post-retirement career?

When researchers ask retirees to describe what they'd like their life to be like five or ten years from now, common themes emerge. Being in love, and being loved—both are at the top of the list. Being happy, having friends they can count on, having family close by—those are mentioned frequently as well. Their "hoped-for future selves" are healthy, but not necessarily rich, it turns out. Why? For most of us, feeling satisfied with the choices we've made is more important than having a lot of money.

Now that you know about making it work, and making it count, you're ready to turn this knowledge into action. Retirement is your last, best opportunity to become the self you want to be.

So during the coming years, every time you must make an important choice, stop and think: will this choice bring me closer to the person I'd like to become? By asking that question, you'll know what to do. The answer is already within you.

A Bit of Business

On pages 223–244, you'll find resources grouped by topic—contact information for agencies and organizations that provide helpful information regarding retirement-related issues (everything from finances and health care to housing and social networking). We've tried to provide as much information as possible (mailing addresses, phone numbers, email, websites, and so on). We've also included an online version of this list in the Resources section of www.aging-wisely.com, and we invite you to check that out as well. The online resource list has two advantages over the printed list at the back of the book. First, the Internet links are "live"—if you click on them, they'll take you directly to the website. Second, unlike the resource list here in the book, we can update our online list as new resources become available, so you'll have access to the most up-to-date information regarding all aspects of aging in place.

Let Us Know. . .

If you found some parts of this book to be especially useful, please let us know. If some parts of the book could be improved, please let us know that, too. We wrote *How to Age in Place* to help, and we want to learn how we can do better. So if you have a moment, please visit our website at www.aging-wisely.com and click on the Contact Us link. We can't respond to every message we receive (though we do try). But we read every one carefully, and take your comments seriously. You have our word on it.

Checklists and Worksheets

Essential and Lifestyle Expenses Worksheet

Accurate financial planning requires that you estimate both your *essential expenses* (those things you can't live without) and your *lifestyle expenses* (those things you enjoy, but could do without if you had to). Unanticipated expenses arise, of course, and you'll need to plan on that. But if you use this worksheet to develop a realistic estimate of your essential and lifestyle expenses, and assume you'll need some extra funds every now and then to pay for the unexpected, you'll have a pretty good handle on your post-retirement finances. Be sure to update this worksheet periodically (once a year is about right for most people), and don't forget to factor in the effects of inflation as you estimate future costs.

Essential Expenses

HOME

Mortgage Fees: $ _____

Rent/Condo Fees: $ _____

Home Repair/Upkeep: $ _____

Lawn Care: $ _____

Snow Removal: $ _____

TAXES

Federal: $ _____

State: $ _____

Local: $ _____

INSURANCE

Health: $ _____

Medigap: $ _____

Long-term Care: $ _____

Auto: $ _____

Homeowners: $ _____

Personal Umbrella: $ _____

SERVICES

Landline Phone: $ _____

Smartphone/Cell Phone: $ _____

Internet: $ _____

Electricity: $ _____

Oil/Gas: $ _____

Water: $ _____

AUTO EXPENSES

Purchase/Replacement: $ _____

Repairs: $ _____

Fees: $ _____

Fuel: $ _____

HEALTH CARE

Medical: $ _____

Dental: $ _____

Vision Care: $ _____

Other: $ _____

Prescription Medications: $ _____

Over-the-Counter Medications: $ _____

MONEY MANAGEMENT

Accountant Fees: $ _____

Financial Planning Fees: $ _____

Bank Fees/Safe Deposit Box: $ _____

REGULAR/PERIODIC PURCHASES

Groceries: $ _____

Clothing and Shoes: $ _____

Home Goods: $ _____

Appliances/Electronics: $ _____

Lifestyle Expenses

Travel: $ _____

Restaurants: $ _____

Hobbies: $ _____

Discretionary Purchases: $ _____

Cable/Satellite Dish: $ _____

Newspaper and Magazine Subscriptions: $ _____

Club/Association Membership Fees: $ _____

Professional Dues: $ _____

Theater/Concerts: $ _____

Family Member Gifts/Support: $ _____

Calculating Your Net Worth

To calculate your net worth, subtract your total liabilities from your total assets. You can calculate net worth for yourself or for you and your partner together. Don't forget to update these figures periodically as circumstances change.

Assets

SAVINGS AND INVESTMENTS

Cash/Cash Equivalents_____

CDs _____

Stocks_____

Bonds_____

Mutual Funds _____

Investment Real Estate _____

RETIREMENT

IRAs _____

Roth IRAs_____

401(k)s / 403(b)s_____

Annuities _____

Pensions _____

Deferred Compensation _____

CASH VALUE

Insurance _____

Home_____

Business _____

Autos _____

Recreational Vehicles _____

Household Items _____

Collectibles _____

OTHER

Partnerships_____

Loans Receivable_____

TOTAL ASSETS _____

Liabilities

MORTGAGES

Mortgage on Primary Residence _____

Other Mortgages_____

OUTSTANDING LOANS

Auto_____

Personal _____

Home Equity_____

Other _____

OTHER MONIES OWED

Unpaid Taxes_____

Unpaid Bills_____

Credit Card Debt _____

Other _____

TOTAL LIABILITIES: _____

_____ (Total Assets)

− _____ (Total Liabilities)

_____

= _____ (Net Worth)

Access-Opportunities-Services (AOS) Worksheet

You can use this worksheet to evaluate access, opportunities, and services for any location where you might choose to age in place (including your current home). You can also use the worksheet to compare different options, and weigh the advantages and limitations of each.

Access

Access involves being able to move around safely, within and outside your home. It also means being able to get to the places you need to be (like doctors' offices), and obtain the things you need to live (like groceries). Here are some key access issues to consider:

HOUSING

❏ Age-appropriate housing available

❏ Neighborhood is safe and well maintained

❏ Living space conforms to principles of universal home design

EMERGENCY SERVICES

❏ Emergency response systems in place, or can be installed

❏ Trauma 1 emergency room nearby

TRANSPORTATION

❏ Public transportation within walking distance

❏ AbleRide/other appointment-based service available

❏ Taxi/car service available

SHOPPING

- ❏ Grocery store within walking distance
- ❏ Clothing store within walking distance
- ❏ Pharmacy within walking distance
- ❏ Household/hardware store within walking distance

HEALTH CARE

- ❏ Appropriate medical care is accessible
- ❏ Appropriate dental care is accessible
- ❏ Other needed health care is accessible (specify)

Opportunities

Being able to do the things you want is the whole point of aging in place. No location is perfect; different areas provide different types of opportunities. Important opportunities come from the following categories:

SOCIAL

- ❏ Senior center nearby
- ❏ Community groups for retirees available
- ❏ Affordable/accessible restaurants nearby

RECREATIONAL

- ❏ Recreational space available and accessible
- ❏ Recreational programming for retirees

CULTURAL

- ❏ Members of one's cultural group live in area
- ❏ Availability of preferred foods and other items

EDUCATIONAL

- ❑ Four-year college or university campus nearby
- ❑ Community college campus nearby
- ❑ Adult education classes available and affordable
- ❑ Lectures and workshops available and affordable

RELIGIOUS/SPIRITUAL

- ❑ Appropriate house of worship nearby
- ❑ Active religious/spiritual community in area

ENGAGEMENT

- ❑ Opportunities for civic engagement are available
- ❑ Opportunities for charitable work are available

Services

Making sure you can obtain the services you need is one of the most significant challenges of aging in place. Here's what you should consider as you evaluate different living options:

HEALTH

- ❑ Physician nearby and accessible
- ❑ Dentist nearby and accessible
- ❑ Hospital nearby and accessible
- ❑ Emergency services in place

SOCIAL

- ❑ Post-retirement job training/retraining is available
- ❑ Assistance in accessing benefits is available
- ❑ Housekeeping assistance is available
- ❑ Check-in services are available

NUTRITION

- ❏ Affordable grocery store nearby
- ❏ Grocery store carries needed items
- ❏ Grocery delivery available
- ❏ Meals on Wheels available

SAFETY ISSUES

- ❏ Area has adequate police protection
- ❏ Neighborhood Watch group exists

LEGAL/FINANCIAL

- ❏ Bank or credit union nearby and accessible
- ❏ Accountant is accessible, or will do home visits
- ❏ Attorney experienced in elder law accessible and affordable

HOME MAINTENANCE

- ❏ Affordable lawn care service available
- ❏ Affordable and reliable snow removal service in area
- ❏ Affordable home repair company in area
- ❏ Affordable plumber/electrician in area

Home Health Care Comparison Checklist

Agency/Provider

AGENCY INFORMATION

- ❏ Well established in area
- ❏ Known by your physician
- ❏ Works with local hospitals
- ❏ Awards from federal or state agencies
- ❏ Censures from federal or state agencies

COST

Total cost per day _____

Amount covered by Medicare _____

Amount covered by Medicaid _____

Amount covered by other insurance _____

Total out-of-pocket costs _____

STAFFING

- ❏ Adequate staffing patterns
- ❏ Guaranteed coverage options
- ❏ Specialists available as needed
- ❏ Emergency plans in place
- ❏ Options available for finding optimal caregiver match

CAREGIVER QUALIFICATIONS

- ❑ All providers trained at accredited institutions
- ❑ Professional providers licensed or certified in their specialties
- ❑ Nonlicensed staff supervised by licensed providers
- ❑ Caregivers experienced with problems like yours

REFERENCES

- ❑ Former clients generally satisfied with agency
- ❑ Former clients generally satisfied with caregivers
- ❑ Caregivers were reliable
- ❑ Caregivers were competent
- ❑ Caregivers were pleasant
- ❑ Problems were resolved successfully
- ❑ Past clients would use agency again
- ❑ Problems reported by past clients

Universal Home Design Checklist

EXTERIOR

- ❏ Low-maintenance exterior for house (vinyl or brick rather than wood or stucco)
- ❏ Deck or patio flush with exterior doorway
- ❏ Low-maintenance shrubs and other plants
- ❏ Plants do not block sightlines to windows and doorways from street
- ❏ Smooth pathways and walkways (no steps)
- ❏ Pathways and walkways are paved (not dirt, grass, or gravel)
- ❏ Entry capable of accommodating access ramp if necessary

GARAGE/CARPORT

- ❏ Covered carports/parking spaces
- ❏ Minimum of 5' access space between vehicle and interior entry in garage
- ❏ Ramp to doorway if garage floor is lower than house floor level

RAMPS (INTERIOR OR EXTERIOR)

- ❏ Maximum slope of 1" rise per foot of ramp length
- ❏ Adequate handrails on both sides of ramp
- ❏ Minimum 2" curbs on both sides of ramp
- ❏ Nonskid surface on ramp
- ❏ Minimum 5' square landing/turnaround area at top of ramp

HALLWAYS, DOORWAYS, AND THRESHOLDS

- ❑ Hallways and doorways at least 36" wide
- ❑ Levered door handles instead of knobs
- ❑ Exterior doorway thresholds no more than $1/2$" high (preferably flush)
- ❑ Interior doorway thresholds no more than $1/4$" high (preferably flush)
- ❑ Peephole at low height on all exterior doors (or standard height plus wheelchair height peepholes)

WINDOWS

- ❑ Lower windowsills to allow clear view from wheelchair
- ❑ Easy-to-operate window hardware
- ❑ Easy-to-operate drape, shade, and blinds hardware

BATHROOMS

- ❑ Lever faucets (or pedal-controlled faucets)
- ❑ Faucet mixers with antiscald valves
- ❑ Stall shower with low threshold and shower seat
- ❑ Ceiling light in shower stall
- ❑ Grab bars at back and sides of shower
- ❑ Toilet $2^{1}/2$" higher than standard toilet
- ❑ Grab bar at side of toilet
- ❑ Toilet-paper holder allows rolls to be changed with one hand
- ❑ Adequate turnaround space for walker or wheelchair (at least 48" by 48")
- ❑ Nonslip flooring
- ❑ No bathroom rug (or rug is secured to the floor)

KITCHEN

- ❑ Lever faucets (or pedal-controlled faucets)
- ❑ Faucet mixers with antiscald valves
- ❑ Cabinets with pull-out shelves and lazy Susans
- ❑ Cooktop with front controls
- ❑ Side-by-side refrigerator
- ❑ Lowered kitchen counters (30" high)
- ❑ Open shelving/cabinets for frequently used items
- ❑ Counter-height microwave oven

LAUNDRY

- ❑ Front-loading washer and dryer
- ❑ Washing machine and dryer 12" to 15" above floor for easier access
- ❑ Laundry chute if multistory home

STAIRWAYS/LIFTS

- ❑ Adequate handrails on both sides of stairways
- ❑ Contrast strips on top and bottom of stairs
- ❑ Nonskid flooring on each step

STORAGE

- ❑ Adjustable rod and shelf heights
- ❑ Lighting in closets with easy-to-operate on/off switch

ELECTRICAL/LIGHTING

- ❑ Light switches at 42" rather than standard 48"
- ❑ Electrical outlets at 18" or 24" rather than standard 12"
- ❑ Easy-to-push "rockers" for light switches
- ❑ Luminous ("night light") light switches
- ❑ No electrical cords/extension cords across open areas of rooms
- ❑ Remote-control (or voice-activated) on/off switches for lights, radios, and televisions

SECURITY

- ❏ Whole-house alarm system (to prevent break-ins)
- ❏ Personal alarm system (for health emergencies)
- ❏ Motion-sensitive exterior lights

FLOORING

- ❏ No area rugs (or area rugs are secured to the floor)
- ❏ Nonslip flooring

HEATING, VENTILATION, AND AIR CONDITIONING

- ❏ Vents positioned low on walls (rather than ceiling vents)
- ❏ Easily accessible filters (may be changed with one hand)
- ❏ Easy-to-read thermostats
- ❏ Programmable thermostats

OVERALL/GENERAL

- ❏ Capacity to adapt ground floor of home for single-level living
- ❏ Contrasting colors to demarcate floors and walls
- ❏ Wide, clutter-free paths through rooms
- ❏ At least one 5' by 5' minimum turnaround space in every room
- ❏ Furniture seating at least 18" off the floor
- ❏ Sturdy arms on chairs
- ❏ Central vacuum system
- ❏ Intercom system

Walkability Checklist

This checklist will help you to evaluate neighborhood walkability and compare walkability in different locations. Each item listed in the first six categories represents a potential problem; the more items you check, the less walkable the neighborhood. The final section allows you to note destinations in each neighborhood that are reachable by walking—another important consideration when evaluating overall walkability.

SIDEWALKS

- ❏ Sidewalks were interrupted (started and stopped)
- ❏ Sidewalks were broken or cracked
- ❏ Metal grates replace large sections of sidewalk
- ❏ One or more curbs too high to step down or up safely
- ❏ Sidewalks were blocked with poles, signs, or other permanent fixtures
- ❏ Sidewalks were blocked by chained bicycles, food carts, or other movable objects
- ❏ Overhanging branches or shrubbery blocking parts of sidewalks
- ❏ Inadequate room for two people to walk side by side
- ❏ Inadequate room for wheelchair during heavy-use times
- ❏ No sidewalks, paths, or walkable shoulders

CROSSINGS

- ❏ Road(s) too wide to cross safely
- ❏ Crossings separated by more than 300 feet
- ❏ Traffic signals did not provide adequate time to cross
- ❏ Traffic signal timing too long (more than two-minute wait to cross)
- ❏ No traffic signals
- ❏ No clearly marked pedestrian crossing areas
- ❏ Pedestrians in crossing areas not easily seen by drivers

- ☐ Parked cars blocking crossing areas
- ☐ Trees, plants, or large vehicles blocking view of traffic
- ☐ No curb ramps
- ☐ Curb ramps inadequate or in need of repair

AUTOMOBILE TRAFFIC

- ☐ Too much traffic
- ☐ Traffic too fast
- ☐ Cars backed out of driveways without looking
- ☐ Cars blocked sidewalk when exiting driveways, garages, or alleys
- ☐ Cars failed to yield to pedestrians
- ☐ Cars intruded upon pedestrians when making right turn on red
- ☐ Drivers sped up to make traffic lights
- ☐ Drivers ignored signs and traffic signals

FOOT TRAFFIC

- ☐ Too much foot traffic to walk safely
- ☐ Pedestrians hurried or rude
- ☐ Bicycles or skateboards maneuvering on sidewalk

SIGNAGE

- ☐ Inadequate signage
- ☐ Signage difficult to decipher
- ☐ Signage not clearly visible to drivers
- ☐ Signage not clearly visible to pedestrians

ATMOSPHERE/AMBIANCE

- ☐ Little or no grass, flowers, bushes, or trees
- ☐ No (or too few) benches/resting places
- ☐ Inadequate separation between traffic and walking area
- ☐ Scary dogs

- ❑ Scary people
- ❑ Not well lighted
- ❑ Dirty (too much litter or trash)
- ❑ Dirty air due to car exhaust
- ❑ Too much honking
- ❑ Too noisy (not honking)

DESTINATIONS REACHABLE BY WALKING (CHECK ALL THAT APPLY)

- ❑ Grocery store
- ❑ Pharmacy
- ❑ Bank/credit union
- ❑ Convenience store
- ❑ House of worship
- ❑ Restaurant(s)
- ❑ Hardware store
- ❑ Library
- ❑ School
- ❑ Park
- ❑ Community pool
- ❑ Senior center
- ❑ Medical building/doctor's office
- ❑ City/town office or municipal building
- ❑ Bus stop
- ❑ Train station
- ❑ Taxi stand

Calories Burned Worksheet

You can use this worksheet to keep a record of your activities and the approximate number of calories burned by each. There are a number of smartphone apps available that provide calorie estimates. (Some will actually track your calorie intake and calories expended, if you input the necessary information.) You can also consult one of the many websites that offer descriptions of the relative value of various calorie-burning activities. Here are two of the more useful ones:

- Harvard Medical School: www.health.harvard.edu/newsweek /Calories-burned-in-30-minutes-of-leisure-and-routine-activities.htm
- The Mayo Clinic: www.mayoclinic.com/health/exercise/SM00109

As we noted in chapter 7, you only need to burn an extra 100 calories per day to lose about a pound per month. And as the list below shows, burning an extra 100 calories a day isn't all that difficult. Always check with your physician before altering your food intake or beginning a new exercise regimen.

Task/Activity	Calories Burned in 30 Minutes for People of Varying Weights (in pounds)		
	130	155	190
Walking (4 mph)	150	185	220
Jogging (< 10 mph)	180	220	265
Dancing	170	210	245
Gardening	135	165	200
Mowing (power)	135	165	200
Mowing (hand)	165	205	245
Raking leaves	120	150	180
Gutter cleaning	150	185	220
Food shopping	100	130	150
Cooking	75	95	110

continued

Calories Burned Worksheet, continued

Task/Activity	Calories Burned in 30 Minutes for People of Varying Weights (in pounds)		
	130	155	190
Office work	45	55	65
Bathing the dog	200	240	280
Playing golf	260	310	360
Miniature golf	180	210	250
Watching TV	20	25	25
Sleeping	20	25	25

Activity	Calories Used	Time Spent	Total Calories Burned
Overall Total			

Reframing: A Worksheet to Accentuate the Positive

When you find yourself overwhelmed by anxiety—obsessing about a task or a situation that's gone wrong—there are things you can do to help quiet the voice in your head, relax, and move on. It's called *reframing*, and it's a well-established psychological strategy. So when your emotions are getting the better of you, ask yourself a series of questions—and answer them honestly. You'll feel better for having done so.

1. What's the worst possible outcome here? Is it really all that bad?

2. Is this actually *my* problem, or one that's been dumped on me?

3. Have I experienced a similar problem in the past? Was I able to handle it?

4. Am I seeing this as an all-or-nothing situation when in fact there is a range of possible outcomes?

5. Am I fretting about something that's outside my control?

6. What if I just do nothing? What will happen then?

7. Is part of my worry the fear that if this works out badly, I'll have failed?

8. Am I doing something I don't want to as a way of getting others to like me?

Checklist: What to Look for in a Nonprofit

Nonprofits vary tremendously with respect to how efficiently they're run and how effectively they fulfill their stated mission. For up-to-date ratings and current information, you can visit nonprofit watchdog websites like www.charitynavigator.org, www.charitywatch.org, and www.greatnonprofits.org.

Here are some indicators of a well-run organization. The more of these you can check, the more efficient and effective the nonprofit.

- ❑ Organization has 501(c)(3) status, signifying that it's a tax-exempt nonprofit organization recognized by the IRS.
- ❑ More than 75 percent of donations go toward charitable work. (Less than 60 percent is a red flag.)
- ❑ Executive compensation is not excessive. ($150,000 per year is about average for top-level executives in nonprofits; somewhat higher in the Northeast and other expensive locales.)
- ❑ Fund-raising and administrative expenses are modest. (10 to 15 percent is good.)
- ❑ Expenses are not increasing significantly each year (definitely not increasing more than the rate of inflation).
- ❑ financial records are accessible and in order. (Transparency is key here—reputable organizations have nothing to hide.)
- ❑ There are independent voting members—people who are not employed or paid by the organization—on the board of directors.
- ❑ Board members are elected by people who are served by the organization.
- ❑ Board minutes are made public (usually on the organization's website).
- ❑ There are no outstanding legal or financial complaints against the organization—and no ongoing legal or financial investigations.
- ❑ Organization does not use high-pressure sales tactics (see sidebar on page 194).

Resource
and Contact
Information

In this section we list key resources, grouped by topic. We've included as much detail as possible for each: mailing addresses, telephone numbers, email links, and website information. Even when addresses and phone numbers change, the website info usually remains the same, so if you have Internet access this is probably the best place to begin. If a particular website doesn't come up when you enter the address, try entering the resource name (for example, National Association of Area Agencies on Aging) into Google. The link to the website should pop right up.

As you'll see, some organizations provide email contact info, some don't, and a few require that email inquiries be submitted through a Contact Us link in the website. Where possible we've provided email contact information; if no email address is provided, contact for that particular organization is limited to phone and postal mail.

AGENCIES ON AGING

Your local Agency on Aging should be listed in the Human Services section of the phone book, or contact the National Association of Area Agencies on Aging.

National Association of Area Agencies on Aging
1730 Rhode Island Avenue, NW
Suite 1200
Washington, DC 20036
202-872-0888
www.n4a.org

AGING IN PLACE

The National Aging in Place Council (NAIPC) is a collaborative group of professional service providers who provide information regarding strategies for aging in place, along with contact information for aging in place professionals grouped by topic (for example, home modification specialists). The website also provides links to regional NAIPC chapters throughout the United States.

National Aging in Place Council
1400 16th Street, NW
Suite 420
Washington, DC 20036
202-939-1770
www.ageinplace.org

ASSISTED LIVING

The Assisted Living Federation of America provides regional listings of accredited senior housing and assisted living facilities, and links to reputable organizations.

Assisted Living Federation of America
1650 King Street
Suite 602
Alexandria, VA 22314
793-894-1805
Multiple email contacts accessed through Contact Us link
www.alfa.org

CAREGIVER RESOURCES/SUPPORT

The three organizations listed below provide a variety of resources for caregivers and family members. Also check out the US Administration on Aging's Federal Eldercare Locator at www.eldercare.gov and the National Clearinghouse for Long Term Care Information at www.longtermcare.gov.

Children of Aging Parents
PO Box 167
Richboro, PA 18954
800-227-7294
www.caps4caregivers.org

Family Caregiver Alliance
785 Market Street
Suite 750
San Francisco, CA 94103
415-434-3388
800-445-8106
info@caregiver.org
www.caregiver.org

National Alliance for Caregiving
4720 Montgomery Lane
Bethesda, MD 20814
301-718-8444
www.caregiving.org

EXERCISE AND FITNESS

The American Senior Fitness Association provides excellent, detailed advice in this area—or check out Sit and Be Fit with Mary Ann Wilson, a nonprofit organization devoted to fitness and healthy aging.

The American Senior Fitness Association
PO Box 2575
New Smyrna Beach, FL 32170
386-423-6634
888-689-6791 (toll free)
asfa@seniorfitness.net
www.seniorfitness.net

Sit and Be Fit
PO Box 8033
Spokane, WA 99203
509-448-9438
sitandbefit@sitandbefit.org
www.sitandbefit.org

FINANCES

Financial Planning Association
7535 East Hampton Avenue
Suite 600
Denver, CO 80231
800-322-4237
www.fpanet.org

National Reverse Mortgage Lenders Association
1400 16th Street, NW
Suite 420
Washington, DC 20036
202-939-1760
www.nrmlaonline.org

Society of Financial Service Professionals
19 Campus Boulevard
Suite 100
Newtown Square, PA 19073
610-526-2500
info@financialpro.org
www.financialpro.org

FUNERAL PLANNING

National Funeral Directors Association
13625 Bishop's Drive
Brookfield, WI 53005
800-228-6332
262-789-1880
nfda@nfda.org
www.nfda.org

GIVING BACK/CHARITABLE OPPORTUNITIES/NONPROFITS

Action Without Borders
302 Fifth Avenue
11th Floor
New York, NY 10001
646-786-6886
www.idealist.org

Charity Navigator
139 Harristown Road
Suite 201
Glen Rock, NJ 07452
201-818-1288
info@charitynavigator.org
www.charitynavigator.org

CharityWatch (formerly the American Institute for Philanthropy)
PO Box 578460
Chicago, IL 60657
773-529-2300
aipmail@charitywatch.org
www.charitywatch.org

Corporation for National & Community Service (Serve.gov)
1201 New York Avenue, NW
Washington, DC 20525
202-606-5000
info@cns.gov
www.nationalservice.gov

Great Nonprofits
PO Box 1133
Palo Alto, CA 94103
650-521-3084
www.greatnonprofits.org

The Mentoring Center (formerly The National Mentoring Partnership)
672 13th Street
Suite 200
Oakland, CA 94612
510-891-0427
www.mentor.org

TESOL International Association (Teachers of English as a Second Language)
1925 Ballenger Avenue
Suite 550
Alexandria, VA 22314
888-547-3369
240-646-7048
info@tesol.org
www.tesol.org

VolunteerMatch
550 Montgomery Street
8th Floor
San Francisco, CA 94111
415-241-6868
www.volunteermatch.org

Volunteers of America
1660 Duke Street
Alexandria, VA 22314
800-899-0089
volunteers@voa.org
www.voa.org

HEALTH

These associations provide information regarding various late-life health problems. The American Medical Association and National Health Information Center also serve as clearinghouses where you can obtain additional resources in these (or other) areas.

Academy of Nutrition and Dietetics (formerly American Dietetic Association)
120 South Riverside Plaza
Suite 2000
Chicago, IL 60606
800-877-1600
312-899-0040
Multiple email contacts accessed through Contact ADA link
www.webdietitians.org

Alzheimer's Association
225 North Michigan Avenue
Floor 17
Chicago, IL 60601
800-272-3900 (24/7 helpline)
312-335-8700
info@alz.org
www.alz.org

American Academy of Ophthalmology
PO Box 7424
San Francisco, CA 94120
415-561-8500
Multiple email contacts accessed through Contact Us link
www.aao.org

American Academy of Physician Assistants
2318 Mill Road
Suite 1300
Alexandria, VA 22314
703-836-2272
aapa@aapa.org
www.aapa.org

American Diabetes Association
1701 North Beauregard Street
Alexandria, VA 22311
800-342-2383
AskADA@diabetes.org
www.diabetes.org

American Heart Association
7272 Greenville Avenue
Dallas, TX 75231
800-242-8721
www.heart.org

American Lung Association
1301 Pennsylvania Avenue, NW
Suite 800
Washington, DC 20004
202-785-3355
www.lung.org

American Medical Association
515 North State Street
Chicago, IL 60654
800-621-8335
No email provided for the public (physicians only)
www.ama-assn.org

American Occupational Therapy Association
4720 Montgomery Lane
Suite 200
Bethesda, MD 20814
301-652-2682
Multiple email contacts accessed through Contact Us link
www.aota.org

American Parkinson Disease Association
135 Parkinson Avenue
Staten Island, NY 10305
800-223-2732
718-981-8001
apda@apdaparkinson.org
www.apdaparkinson.org

American Physical Therapy Association
1111 North Fairfax Street
Alexandria, VA 22314
703-684-2782
800-999-2782
www.apta.org

American Podiatric Medical Association
9312 Old Georgetown Road
Bethesda, MD 20814
315-581-9200
www.apma.org

Arthritis Foundation
1330 West Peachtree Street
Suite 100
Atlanta, GA 30309
404-872-7100
Multiple email contacts, organized by region
www.arthritis.org

National Association of Professional Geriatric Care Managers
3275 West Ina Road
Suite 130
Tucson, AZ 85741
520-881-8008
www.caremanager.org

National Cancer Institute
6116 Executive Boulevard
Suite 300
Bethesda, MD 20892
800-422-6237
www.nci.nih.gov

National Institute of Neurological Disorders and Stroke
NIH Neurological Institute
PO Box 5801
Bethesda, MD 20824
800-352-9424
301-496-5751
www.ninds.nih.gov

National Institute on Deafness and Other Communication
Disorders
Office of Health Communication and Public Liaison
31 Center Drive, MSC 2320
Bethesda, MD 20892
301-496-7243
301-341-1055 (TTY)
nidcdinfo@nidcd.nih.gov
www.nidcd.nih.gov

National Kidney Foundation
30 East 33rd Street
New York, NY 10016
800-622-9010
www.kidney.org

National Osteoporosis Foundation
1150 17th Street, NW Suite 850
Washington, DC 20036
800-231-4222
www.nof.org

Urology Care Foundation (official foundation of the American
Urological Association)
1000 Corporate Boulevard
Linthicum, MD 21090
410-689-3700
info@urologycarefoundation.org
www.urologyhealth.org

HEALTHY EATING

WebMD has a good section on eating for longevity. Also check the Healthy Eating for Older Adults section of the Academy of Nutrition and Dietetics website.

Academy of Nutrition and Dietetics
120 South Riverside Plaza
Suite 2000
Chicago, IL 60606
800-877-1600
312-899-0040
Multiple email addresses accessed through Contact Us link
www.eatright.org

HOSPICE

You can learn more about hospice philosophy and practice through these organizations, which also provide links for local hospice contact information.

American Academy of Hospice and Palliative Medicine
4700 West Lake Drive
Glenview, IL 60025
847-375-4712
info@aahpm.org
www.aahpm.org

Compassion & Choices
PO Box 101810
Denver, CO 80250
800-247-7421
Multiple email contacts accessed through staff members list
www.compassionandchoices.org

Hospice Foundation of America
1710 Rhode Island Avenue, NW
Suite 400
Washington, DC 20036
202-457-5811
800-854-3402
hfaoffice@hospicefoundation.org
www.hospicefoundation.org

HOUSING

The National Association of Home Builders (NAHB) provides information regarding housing laws, regulations, and ethics, as well as links to Certified Aging in Place Specialists. AbleData provides accessibility and home modification information, while Seniornet provides technology resources (including user-friendly Internet "how to" instructions). The National Shared Housing Resource Center provides links to websites of seven regional centers in the United States and one international resource center, with name of director, phone, and email contact (through the About Us link); you can also click the Program Directory link to see a listing of shared housing programs by state.

AbleData
8630 Fenton Street
Suite 930
Silver Spring, MD 20910
301-608-8998
800-227-0216
abledata@macrointernational.com
www.abledata.com

National Association of Home Builders (NAHB)
1201 15th Street, NW
Washington, DC 20005
202-266-8200
800-368-5242
www.nahb.org

National Shared Housing Resource Center
Separate phone and email contacts for seven regional offices
info@nationalsharedhousing.org
www.nationalsharedhousing.org

Seniornet
12801 Worldgate Drive
Suite 500
Herndon, Virginia 20170
571-203-7100
Multiple email contacts accessed through Contact Us link
www.seniornet.com

IN-HOME CARE

These resources provide local contact information as well as accreditation information for home care agencies and providers (including summaries of problems and deficiencies).

National Association for Home Care & Hospice
228 Seventh Street, SE
Washington, DC 20003
202-547-7424
Multiple email contacts accessed through Contact Us link
www.nahc.org

Visiting Nurse Associations of America
900 19th Street, NW
Suite 200
Washington, DC 20006
202-384-1420
vnaa@vnaa.org
www.vnaa.org

INSURANCE INFORMATION

The Health Insurance Association of America is a national advocacy and consumer protection organization; A. M. Best and Standard & Poor's provide useful, up-to-date ratings of private insurance companies.

A. M. Best Company
Ambest Road
Oldwick, NJ 08858
908-439-2200
Email contact limited to members/subscribers
www.ambest.com

America's Health Insurance Plans (formerly Health Insurance Association of America)
601 Pennsylvania Avenue, NW
South Building, Suite 500
Washington, DC 20004
202-778-3200
ahip@ahip.org
www.hiaa.org

Standard & Poor's Insurance Rating Services
55 Water Street
New York, NY 10041
877-772-5436
www.standardandpoors.com

LEGAL ISSUES

The Pension Rights Center can provide information and guidance regarding pensioners' legal rights (particularly helpful if a dispute should arise).

American Bar Association
Commission on Law and Aging
740 15th Street, NW
Washington, DC 20005
800-285-2221 (toll-free)
202-662-1000
aging@americanbar.org
www.americanbar.org/groups/law_aging

National Academy of Elder Law Attorneys
1604 North Country Club Road
Tucson, AZ, 85716
520-881-4005
Multiple email contacts accessed through Contact Us link
www.naela.org

Pension Rights Center
1350 Connecticut Avenue, NW
Suite 206
Washington, DC 20036
888-420-6550 (toll-free)
202-296-3776
www.pensionrights.org

MEALS ON WHEELS

Meals on Wheels Association of America
203 South Union Street
Alexandria, VA 22314
888-998-6325 (toll-free)
mowaa@mowaa.org
www.mowaa.org

MEDICARE, MEDICAID, AND SOCIAL SECURITY

You can obtain contact information for your state Medicare office by looking in the Government Offices section of the phone book. Medicaid information is usually listed in the Human Services section of the phone book. If the information is not listed, try contacting CMS.gov directly. Phone contact with the Center for Medicare and Medicaid Services should be initiated with one of their regional offices; contact information is on the website.

Center for Medicare and Medicaid Services
7500 Security Boulevard
Baltimore, MD 21244
Multiple web-based email links
www.cms.gov

Medicare
800-633-4227 (main number)
800-638-6833 (general information hotline)
Multiple web-based email links
www.medicare.gov

Social Security Administration
800-772-1213
Web-based email link accessed through Online Feedback Form
www.ssa.gov

MEDICATION

The Institute for Safe Medication Practices (ISMP) website not only has a tool to flag harmful drug interactions, but also provides a wealth of information regarding safe medication practices (up-to-date drug safety alerts, storage of different medications, and so on).

Institute for Safe Medication Practices (ISMP)
200 Lakeside Drive
Suite 200
Horsham, PA 19044
215-947-7797
www.ismp.org

MENTAL HEALTH

These organizations provide information regarding mental health problems, and their membership lists include licensed providers in most every region of the country. The Geriatric Mental Health Foundation is a nonprofit organization devoted to promoting mental health and healthy aging in older adults, and providing support to family members.

American Psychiatric Association
1400 K Street, NW
Washington, DC 20005
202-682-6000
apa@psych.org
www.psych.org

American Psychological Association
750 First Street, NE
Washington, DC 20002
800-374-2721
202-336-5500
Multiple email contacts accessed through Contact Us link
www.apa.org

Geriatric Mental Health Foundation
7910 Woodmont Avenue
Suite 1050
Bethesda, MD 20814
301-654-7850
web@GMHFonline.org
www.gmhfonline.org

National Association of Social Workers
750 First Street, NE
Suite 700
Washington, DC 20002
202-408-8600
Multiple email contacts accessed through Contact NASW link
www.naswdc.org

NATIONAL AGING ADVOCACY GROUPS

There are several nationwide advocacy groups, as well as groups for people
of different racial, ethnic, and religious backgrounds.

American Association of Retired Persons
601 E Street, NW
Washington, DC 20049
888-687-2277 (toll free)
member@aarp.org
www.aarp.org

B'nai B'rith
2020 K Street NW
7th Floor
Washington, DC 20006
202-857-6600
Multiple email contacts accessed through Contact Us link
www.bnaibrith.org

Catholic Charities USA
2050 Ballenger Avenue
Suite 400
Alexandria, VA 22314
703-549-1390
info@catholiccharitiesusa.org
www.catholiccharitiesusa.org

National Asian Pacific Center on Aging
Melbourne Tower, Suite 914
1511 Third Avenue
Seattle, WA 98101
800-336-2722 (English)
800-582-4218 (Chinese)
800-582-4259 (Korean)
800-582-4336 (Vietnamese)
www.napca.org

National Caucus and Center on Black Aged
1220 L Street
Suite 800
Washington, DC 20005
202-637-8400
support@ncba-aged.org
www.ncba-aged.org

National Council on Aging
1901 L Street NW
4th Floor
Washington, DC 20036
202-479-1200
www.ncoa.org

National Hispanic Council on Agng
The Walker Building
734 15th Street, NW
Suite 1050
Washington, DC 20005
202-347-9733
nhcoa@nhcoa.org
www.nhcoa.org

National Indian Council on Aging
10501 Montgomery Boulevard NE
Suite 210
Albuquerque, NM 87111
505-292-2001
www.nicoa.org

National Institute on Aging
31 Center Drive, MSC 2292
Bethesda, MD 20892
800-222-2225 (toll-free)
Multiple email contacts accessed through Contact Us link
www.nih.gov/nia

SEXUALITY

The National Institute on Aging (see above) has an excellent section on sexuality and aging; check out the Sexuality in Later Life section of the website. Ditto for WebMD. The National Coalition for LGBT Health provides good resources in this area as well.

National Coalition for LGBT Health
1325 Massachusetts Avenue, NW
Suite 705
Washington, DC 20005
202-558-6828
coalition@lgbthealth.net
www.lgbthealth.webolutionary.com

SOCIAL NETWORKING

There are many social networking sites aimed specifically at retirement-age folks; it doesn't take long to build a profile and begin to connect with others. Among the best (most well-run, user-friendly) sites are these:

AARP Online Community
www.aarp.org/onlinecommunity
A bit more limited than some of the others, but integrated with other AARP functions and services, and accessible through the AARP website.

Genkvetch Social Networking
www.genkvetch.com
Despite the name (which we love), it's open to people of all faiths—and also very easy to use.

My Boomer Place
www.myboomerplace.com
Among the simplest sites to get started with if you're not a savvy web user.

TRAVEL

Reputable organizations include Senior Tours and Road Scholar.

Road Scholar (formerly Elderhostel)
11 Avenue de Lafayette
Boston, MA 02111
800-454-5768
registration@roadscholar.org
www.roadscholar.org

Senior Tours
508 Irvington Road
Drexel Hill, PA 19026
800-277-1100
info@seniortours.com
www.seniortours.com

VETERANS' BENEFITS

Information regarding veterans' benefits can be obtained through the Veterans Affairs website (www.va.gov) or by calling 800-827-1000. Contact information for local veterans' services (including local VA contact information) is usually listed in the Human Services section of the phone book (look under "Veterans").

WALKABILITY/ACCESSIBILITY

Check out the National Highway Traffic Safety Administration website for information regarding non-car driving options and regulations (go to www.nhtsa.gov and search using the terms NEV or LSV). The US Access Board provides information regarding accessibility laws and regulations in a wide variety of areas.

US Access Board
1331 F Street, NW
Suite 1000
Washington, DC 20004
800-872-2253
info@access-board.gov
www.access-board.gov

WELLNESS

National Wellness Institute
PO Box 827
1300 College Court
Stevens Point, WI 54481
715-342-2969
nwi@nationalwellness.org
www.nationalwellness.org

Wellness.com
6965 El Camino Real
Suite 542
Carlsbad, CA 92009
800-686-0988
www.wellness.com

About the Authors

Drs. Languirand and Bornstein coauthored *When Someone You Love Needs Nursing Home, Assisted Living, or In-Home Care* (Newmarket Press, 2002), which received the 2003 Caregiver Friendly Award from the National Association of Caregivers. They are also the authors of *Healthy Dependency: Leaning on Others without Losing Yourself* (Newmarket Press, 2003). Drs. Languirand and Bornstein have extensive media experience, with national television appearances on The Discovery Channel and CNN *Headline News*; local television appearances in Philadelphia, Chicago, and Washington, DC; interviews on National Public Radio and other regional and national outlets; interactive chats on WebMD; and print coverage in the *New York Times, Chicago Sun Times, San Francisco Chronicle, Atlanta Constitution*, and *Psychology Today*.

Mary A. Languirand received her PhD in clinical psychology from the State University of New York at Buffalo in 1987, and completed an internship in clinical geropsychology at the R. H. Hutchings Psychiatric Center in Syracuse, New York. Dr. Languirand is coauthor of *The Thinking Skills Workbook* (Charles C. Thomas, 1980, 1984, 2000), a treatment manual for cognitive remediation in older adults. She now practices full-time in Long Island, New York, providing clinical services to individuals and families, and consulting to multidisciplinary treatment teams in skilled nursing facilities.

Robert F. Bornstein received his PhD in clinical psychology from the State University of New York at Buffalo in 1986, completed an internship at the Upstate Medical Center in Syracuse, New York, and is professor of psychology at Adelphi University. Dr. Bornstein has published more than two hundred articles and book chapters on personality dynamics, diagnosis, assessment, and treatment. His research has been funded by grants from the National Institute of Mental Health and the National Science Foundation, and he received the American Psychological Association's 2005 Theodore Millon Award for Excellence in Personality Research.

Index